The Open University

Using Mathematics

Handbook

About this course

This course, MST121 *Using Mathematics*, and the courses MU120 *Open Mathematics* and MS221 *Exploring Mathematics* provide a flexible means of entry to university-level mathematics. Further details may be obtained from the address below.

MST121 uses the software program Mathcad (MathSoft, Inc.) and other software to investigate mathematical and statistical concepts and as a tool in problem solving. This software is provided as part of the course.

This publication forms part of an Open University course. Details of this and other Open University courses can be obtained from the Student Registration and Enquiry Service, The Open University, PO Box 197, Milton Keynes MK7 6BJ, United Kingdom: tel. +44 (0)845 300 6090, email general-enquiries@open.ac.uk

Alternatively, you may visit the Open University website at http://www.open.ac.uk where you can learn more about the wide range of courses and packs offered at all levels by The Open University.

To purchase a selection of Open University course materials visit http://www.ouw.co.uk, or contact Open University Worldwide, Walton Hall, Milton Keynes MK7 6AA, United Kingdom, for a brochure: tel. +44 (0)1908 858793, fax +44 (0)1908 858787, email ouw-customer-services@open.ac.uk

The Open University, Walton Hall, Milton Keynes, MK7 6AA.

First published 1997. Second edition 2004. Third edition 2008. Reprinted 2008.

Edited, designed and typeset by The Open University, using the Open University TEX System.

Printed in the United Kingdom by Cambrian Printers, Aberystwyth.

ISBN 978 0 7492 2944 3

6.2

Contents

If you are taking MST121 and MS221 together, then we suggest that you use the MS221 Handbook for both courses.

The Greek alphabet

A	α	alpha	N	ν	nu
B	β	beta	Ξ	ξ	xi
Γ	γ	gamma	O	o	omicron
Δ	δ	delta	Π	π	pi
E	ε	epsilon	P	ρ	rho
Z	ζ	zeta	Σ	σ	sigma
H	η	eta	T	τ	tau
Θ	θ	theta	Y	υ	upsilon
I	ι	iota	Φ	ϕ	phi
K	κ	kappa	X	χ	chi
Λ	λ	lamda	Ψ	ψ	psi
M	μ	mu	Ω	ω	omega

SI units

The International System of units (SI units) is an internationally agreed set of units and symbols for measuring physical quantities.

Some of these are base units, such as

metre	symbol	m	(measurement of length),
second	symbol	s	(measurement of time),
kilogram	symbol	kg	(measurement of mass).

Prefixes may be added to units. Commonly used prefixes are

c	centi	or	10^{-2}	(e.g. centimetre, cm),
m	milli	or	10^{-3}	(e.g. millisecond, ms),
μ	micro	or	10^{-6}	(e.g. microsecond, μs),
k	kilo	or	10^{3}	(e.g. kilogram, kg),
M	mega	or	10^{6}	(e.g. megagram, Mg).

There are also derived units, which are used for quantities whose measurement combines base units in some way. Some of these are

area	m^2	(metres squared or square metres),
volume	m^3	(metres cubed or cubic metres),
velocity	$m\,s^{-1}$	(metres per second),
acceleration	$m\,s^{-2}$	(metres per second per second).

Mathematical modelling

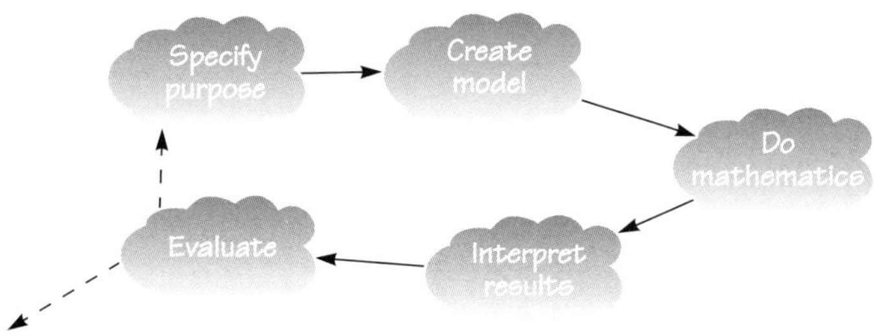

Some useful graphs

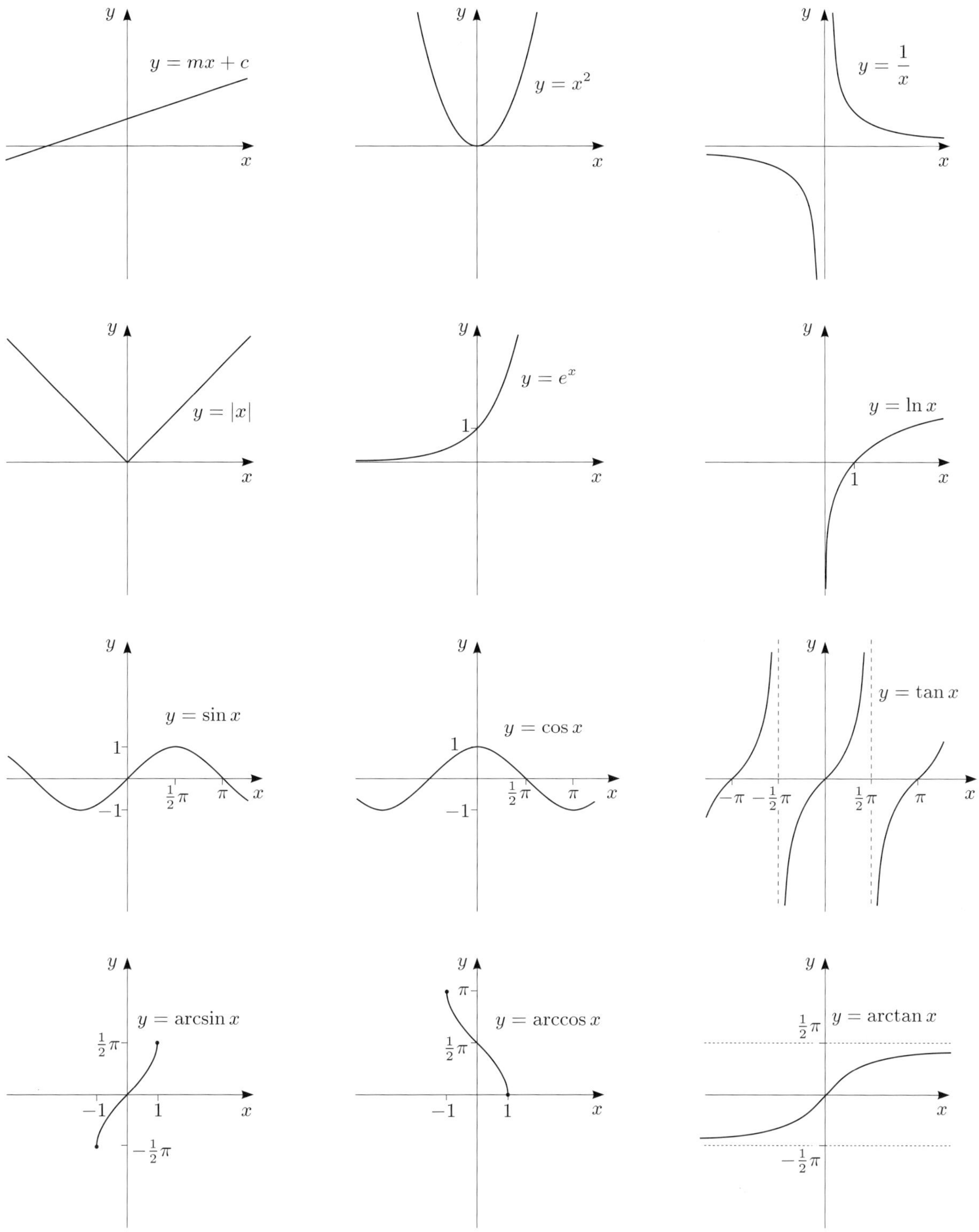

Notation

Some of the notation used in the course is listed below. The right-hand column gives the chapter and page of MST121 where the symbol is first used.

$\mathbb{N}$	the set of natural numbers: $1, 2, 3, \ldots$	**A0 23**
$\mathbb{Z}$	the set of integers: $\ldots, -3, -2, -1, 0, 1, 2, 3, \ldots$	**A0 23**
$\mathbb{Q}$	the set of rational numbers, that is, numbers of the form p/q where p and q are integers, $q \neq 0$	**A0 23**
$\mathbb{R}$	the set of real numbers	**A0 23**
$>$	greater than	**A0 25**
$<$	less than	**A0 25**
$\geq$	greater than or equal to	**A0 25**
$\leq$	less than or equal to	**A0 25**
a^n	a to the power n	**A0 26**
$\sqrt{a}$	the non-negative square root of a, where $a \geq 0$	**A0 26**
$\sqrt[n]{a}$	the nth root of a, where $a \geq 0$	**A0 26**
a^{-n}	$1/a^n$, where $a \neq 0$	**A0 26**
$a^{m/n}$	$\sqrt[n]{a^m}$ (or $(\sqrt[n]{a})^m$), where $n > 0$ and $a \geq 0$	**A3 27**
a_n	the term of a sequence with subscript n, or the sequence whose general term is a_n	**A1 7**
∞	infinity	**A1 33**
$a_n \to l$ as $n \to \infty$	used to describe the long-term behaviour of sequences; the arrow is read as 'tends to'	**A1 33**
(x, y)	the Cartesian coordinates of a point, where x is the displacement along the horizontal axis and y is the displacement along the vertical axis	**A2 6**
$\simeq$	approximately equal to	**A2 18**
$\sin^2 \theta$	$(\sin \theta)^2$; a similar notation is used for other powers and other trigonometric functions	**A2 34**
f	a function	**A3 6**
$f(x) = \ldots$	specifies (in terms of x) the rule of the function f	**A3 6**
$[a, b]$	the interval consisting of the set of all numbers between a and b, including a and b themselves $a \leq x \leq b$	**A3 7**
(a, b)	the interval consisting of the set of all numbers between a and b, but not including a and b themselves $a < x < b$	**A3 7**
$[a, b)$	the interval where the endpoint a is included but b is not; similarly $(a, b]$ includes b but not a $a \leq x < b$	**A3 8**
(a, ∞)	the interval consisting of all numbers greater than a $a < x$	**A3 8**
$\longmapsto$	'maps to' for variables; used to specify the rule of a function, for example, $x \longmapsto e^x$	**A3 9**
$\longrightarrow$	'maps to' for sets; used in functions to show the domain mapping to the codomain, for example, $[0, 4] \longrightarrow [0, 16]$	**A3 9**
$\lvert x \rvert$	the modulus (magnitude or absolute value) of the real number x	**A3 13**

e	the base for the natural logarithm function and the exponential function; $e = 2.718\,281\ldots$	**A3 33**
exp	the exponential function	**A3 34**
f^{-1}	the inverse function of the one-one function f	**A3 37**
$\arccos x$	the angle in the interval $[0, \pi]$ whose cosine is x	**A3 41**
$\arcsin x$	the angle in the interval $[-\frac{1}{2}\pi, \frac{1}{2}\pi]$ whose sine is x	**A3 40**
$\arctan x$	the angle in the interval $(-\frac{1}{2}\pi, \frac{1}{2}\pi)$ whose tangent is x	**A3 41**
$\log_a$	the logarithm function to the base a	**A3 42**
ln	the natural logarithm function, that is, $\log_e$ where $e = 2.718\,281\ldots$	**A3 44**
$\sum_{i=1}^{n} a_i$	the sum $a_1 + a_2 + \cdots + a_n$	**B1 11**
$\lim_{n\to\infty} a_n$	the limit of the convergent sequence a_n	**B1 42**
$\sum_{i=1}^{\infty} a_i$	the infinite sum $a_1 + a_2 + \cdots$	**B1 48**
$\mathbf{A}$	a matrix	**B2 19**
$\mathbf{AB}$	the product of the matrices $\mathbf{A}$ and $\mathbf{B}$	**B2 19**
$\mathbf{A}^n$	the nth power of the square matrix $\mathbf{A}$	**B2 21**
$\mathbf{A} + \mathbf{B}$	the sum of the matrices $\mathbf{A}$ and $\mathbf{B}$	**B2 22**
$k\mathbf{A}$	the scalar multiple of the matrix $\mathbf{A}$ by the real number k	**B2 23**
$\mathbf{A} - \mathbf{B}$	the difference of the matrices $\mathbf{A}$ and $\mathbf{B}$	**B2 23**
a_{ij}	the element in the ith row and jth column of the matrix $\mathbf{A}$	**B2 24**
$\mathbf{v}$	a vector	**B2 26**
v_i	the ith component of the vector $\mathbf{v}$	**B2 26**
$\mathbf{I}$	the identity matrix	**B2 35**
$\mathbf{A}^{-1}$	the inverse of the invertible matrix $\mathbf{A}$	**B2 36**
$\det \mathbf{A}$	the determinant of the square matrix $\mathbf{A}$	**B2 38**
$\mathbf{Ax} = \mathbf{b}$	the matrix form of a pair of simultaneous linear equations	**B2 41**
$\mathbf{0}$	the zero vector	**B3 8**
$\mathbf{i}$	the Cartesian unit vector $\begin{pmatrix}1\\0\end{pmatrix}$	**B3 8**
$\mathbf{j}$	the Cartesian unit vector $\begin{pmatrix}0\\1\end{pmatrix}$	**B3 8**
$\lvert\mathbf{a}\rvert$	the magnitude of the vector $\mathbf{a}$	**B3 10**
$\overrightarrow{PQ}$	the displacement vector from P to Q	**B3 12**
$\overrightarrow{OQ}$	the position vector of Q	**B3 12**
$\mathbf{a} = a_1\mathbf{i} + a_2\mathbf{j}$	the component form of the vector $\mathbf{a}$	**B3 16**
g	the magnitude of the acceleration due to gravity	**B3 40**
$\mathbf{W}$	weight (a vector)	**B3 40**
$\mathbf{T}$	tension (a vector)	**B3 41**
$\mathbf{N}$	normal reaction (a vector)	**B3 41**
f'	the (first) derived function of f	**C1 13**

$f'(x)$	the (first) derivative of the function f at the point x	**C1 13**
f''	the second derived function of f	**C1 28**
$f''(x)$	the second derivative of the function f at the point x	**C1 28**
$\dfrac{dy}{dx}$	the (first) derivative of y with respect to x (Leibniz notation)	**C1 41**
$\dfrac{d^2y}{dx^2}$	the second derivative of y with respect to x (Leibniz notation)	**C1 42**
$\dfrac{d}{dx}(y)$	a variation of $\dfrac{dy}{dx}$	**C1 43**
$\dfrac{d}{dx}(f(x))$	a variation of the Leibniz notation for $f'(x)$	**C1 43**
$\dot{s}$	the (first) derivative of s with respect to t, where t is time (Newton's notation)	**C1 43**
$\ddot{s}$	the second derivative of s with respect to t, where t is time (Newton's notation)	**C1 43**
$\int f(x)\,dx$	the indefinite integral of $f(x)$ with respect to x	**C2 8**
$\int f$	the indefinite integral of the function f	**C2 8**
$\int_a^b f(x)\,dx$	the definite integral of $f(x)$ from a to b	**C2 41**
$\int_a^b f$	the definite integral of the function f from a to b	**C2 41**
$[F(x)]_a^b$	$F(b) - F(a)$	**C2 41**
$y(a) = b$	shorthand for the initial condition $y = b$ when $x = a$	**C3 10**
$P(E)$	the probability that the event E occurs	**D1 10**
$P(X = j)$	the probability that a random variable X takes the value j	**D1 37**
μ	the mean of a probability distribution, or a population mean	**D1 43** **D2 23**
$\overline{x}$	the sample mean	**D2 21**
s	the sample standard deviation	**D2 25**
σ	the standard deviation of a probability distribution, or a population standard deviation	**D2 24**
SE	a standard error, that is, the standard deviation of a sampling distribution	**D3 14** **D4 20**
ESE	an estimated standard error	**D4 22**
$Q1$	the lower quartile	**D4 9**
$Q3$	the upper quartile	**D4 9**
H_0	the null hypothesis of a hypothesis test	**D4 18**
H_1	the alternative hypothesis of a hypothesis test	**D4 18**

Glossary

Below is a glossary of terms used in MST121. First the definition of the term is given, then the page in this handbook where more detail can be found, and finally the chapter and page of MST121 where the term is first used.

absolute value (of a real number) See *modulus (of a real number x).*

acceleration The rate of change of velocity. **B3 40**

acceleration due to gravity The magnitude, g, of the acceleration with which an object falls. On Earth, $g = 9.8\ \mathrm{m\ s^{-2}}$. **B3 40**

alternative hypothesis The hypothesis that is accepted at the end of a hypothesis test when the null hypothesis is rejected. 48 **D4 18**

arbitrary constant See *constant of integration.*

arccosine The inverse function of the cosine function with domain restricted to $[0, \pi]$. 30 **A3 41**

arcsine The inverse function of the sine function with domain restricted to $[-\frac{1}{2}\pi, \frac{1}{2}\pi]$. 30 **A3 40**

arctangent The inverse function of the tangent function with domain restricted to $(-\frac{1}{2}\pi, \frac{1}{2}\pi)$. 30 **A3 41**

arithmetic mean The arithmetic mean (or average) of a set of n numbers is the sum of the numbers divided by n. **A1 14**

arithmetic sequence A sequence in which each term (apart from the first) is obtained by adding a fixed number to the previous term. 26 **A1 14**

asymptote A line which a curve approaches (arbitrarily closely) far from the origin. **A3 11**

batch size The number of values in a batch of data. 47 **D4 9**

bearing A direction given as either North or South followed by an angle (up to 90°) towards the East or West. **B3 24**

bimodal See *mode.*

boxplot A diagram consisting of a box and whiskers, which displays the median, the quartiles and the minimum and maximum values in a batch of data. 47 **D4 8**

calculus The branch of mathematics which includes the study of differentiation and integration. **C1 4**

carrying capacity See *equilibrium population level.*

Cartesian coordinate system Cartesian coordinates (x, y) specify the position of a point in a plane relative to two perpendicular axes, the x-axis (horizontal) and the y-axis (vertical). **A2 6**

Cartesian unit vectors The vectors $\mathbf{i} = \begin{pmatrix} 1 \\ 0 \end{pmatrix}$ and $\mathbf{j} = \begin{pmatrix} 0 \\ 1 \end{pmatrix}$. 36 **B3 16**

chaotic sequence A sequence displaying apparently unstructured behaviour. 31 **B1 40**

chord A line segment joining two points on a curve. **C1 9**

circle The set of points in a plane that are a fixed distance from a specified point in the plane.	27	**A2**	**20**
closed form A formula that defines a sequence a_n in terms of the subscript n. It should be accompanied by a statement of the appropriate range for n.	26	**A1**	**8**
codomain A set containing all the outputs of a function. See also *function*.		**A3**	**9**
coefficient matrix The square matrix used when a pair of simultaneous linear equations are written in matrix form.	35	**B2**	**40**
coefficient (of a term) The factor by which the term is multiplied in a particular product.		**A0**	**31**
column (of a matrix) See *matrix*.			
common difference The difference between any two successive terms in an arithmetic sequence.	26	**A1**	**14**
common logarithm The logarithm function with base 10.		**A3**	**44**
common ratio The ratio of any two successive terms in a geometric sequence.	26	**A1**	**19**
completed-square form The completed-square form of $x^2 + 2px$ is $(x+p)^2 - p^2$.	27	**A2**	**26**
component form (of a vector) The description of a vector $\mathbf{a}$ in terms of the Cartesian unit vectors $\mathbf{i}$ and $\mathbf{j}$: $\mathbf{a} = a_1\mathbf{i} + a_2\mathbf{j}$.	36	**B3**	**16**
component (of a vector) See *vector*.			
composite function A function k with rule of the form $k(x) = g(f(x))$.		**C1**	**48**
confidence interval An interval of plausible values for a population parameter.	47	**D3**	**19**
constant (1) A significant number; for example π.		**A0**	**28**
constant (2) A term in a mathematical expression, whose value does not change during a particular calculation.		**A1**	**14**
constant function A function f with rule of the form $f(x) = c$, where c is a constant.		**C1**	**35**
constant of integration The constant c in the indefinite integral $F(x) + c$.	40	**C2**	**8**
constant sequence A sequence in which each term has the same value.		**A1**	**16**
continuous function Informally, a function is said to be continuous if its graph can be drawn without removing the pen from the paper.		**A3**	**49**
continuous model A model (or representation) in which the associated quantity or quantities can vary throughout some interval of the real line.		**A3**	**49**
continuous variable A variable that can take any value in an interval of the real line.		**A3**	**49**

convergent sequence A sequence that settles down in the long term to values that are effectively constant. Such a sequence is said to converge. See also *limit (of a sequence)*. 32 **B1 42**

cosecant (of an angle θ) The cosecant of θ is $1/\sin\theta$, provided that $\sin\theta \neq 0$. **A2 36**

cosine (of an angle θ) The first coordinate of the point P on the circumference of the unit circle, centre O, where the angle between the positive x-axis and the line segment OP is θ. By convention, angles are measured positively in an anticlockwise direction from the positive x-axis. 27 **A2 33**

Cosine Rule A rule that relates three sides and one angle of a triangle. 37 **B3 34**

cotangent (of an angle θ) The cotangent of θ is $1/\tan\theta$, provided that $\tan\theta \neq 0$. **A2 36**

cubic expression An expression of the form $ax^3 + bx^2 + cx + d$, where $a \neq 0$. **A3 47**

cycling (of a sequence) The behaviour of a sequence that takes a number of different but repeating values; for example, in a 2-cycle the sequence settles to a pattern of alternating between two values. 31 **B1 40**

decay constant The positive constant k in the first-order differential equation $dm/dt = -km$, used to model radioactive decay. 43 **C3 26**

decreasing function A real function f with the property that for all x_1, x_2 in the domain of f, if $x_1 < x_2$, then $f(x_1) > f(x_2)$. 29 **A3 36**

decreasing on an interval A function f is decreasing on an interval I if, for all x_1, x_2 in I, if $x_1 < x_2$, then $f(x_1) > f(x_2)$. 39 **C1 23**

definite integral (of a function $f(x)$ from a to b) The definite integral of a continuous function f from a to b, denoted by $\int_a^b f(x)\,dx$, is $[F(x)]_a^b = F(b) - F(a)$, where F is any integral of f. 40 **C2 41**

degree of a polynomial For a polynomial in x, the highest power of x with a non-zero coefficient. **A3 47**

dependent variable A variable whose value depends on the value of another variable (or variables). **A0 28** **D4 38**

derivative (of a function f at a point x) The gradient of the graph of f at the point $(x, f(x))$, denoted by $f'(x)$. 38 **C1 14**

derived function (of a function f) The function f' defined by the process of differentiation. 38 **C1 14**

determinant (of a matrix) The determinant of the 2×2 matrix $\begin{pmatrix} a & b \\ c & d \end{pmatrix}$ is $ad - bc$. 35 **B2 38**

deviation The deviation of a value x from the population mean μ is $x - \mu$; the deviation of a value x from the sample mean $\overline{x}$ is $x - \overline{x}$. **D2 24**

differential equation An equation that relates an independent variable, x say, a dependent variable, y say, and one or more derivatives of y with respect to x. 42 **C3 6**

differentiation (of a function f) The process of finding the derivative $f'(x)$. 38 **C1 14**

direct integration A method for solving differential equations of the form $dy/dx = f(x)$. 42 **C3 11**

direction field The association, arising from a differential equation, of a gradient with each point (x, y) in a given domain, often represented by a collection of short line segments. **C3 38**

direction (of a vector) The angle θ, measured anticlockwise, that an arrow representing the vector makes with the positive x-direction. 36 **B3 11**

discrete model A model (or representation) in which the associated quantity or quantities can only take separated values. **A3 49**

discrete variable A variable that can only take on values in a separated set, such as the integers. **A3 49**

displacement (vector) The displacement vector from P to Q is represented by the arrow with its tail at P and its tip at Q. **B3 12**

distance The distance of a particle from the origin is a measure of how far it is from the origin, irrespective of direction. 41 **C2 26**

domain (of a function) The set of allowable input values for a function. See also *function*. 28 **A3 6**

doubling time The time that it takes for a population to double in size from any starting value. 43 **C3 32**

element (of a matrix) See *matrix*.

equal matrices Two matrices are equal if they are of the same size and all their corresponding elements agree. **B2 18**

Equilibrium Condition for forces The relationship between the forces acting on an object at rest. 37 **B3 42**

equilibrium population level The population size at which the proportionate growth rate is zero; that is, the size at which the population remains constant. It is represented by the parameter E in the logistic recurrence relation. 31 **B1 32**

estimated standard error A value used to estimate the standard deviation of a sampling distribution. 48 **D4 22**

Euler's method A numerical method for solving initial-value problems of the form $dy/dx = f(x, y)$, $y(x_0) = y_0$. 44 **C3 39**

explanatory variable When investigating the relationship between two variables, the variable whose values 'explain' the values taken by the dependent variable. **D4 38**

explicit solution (of a differential equation) A solution written in the form $y = F(x)$, where F is a known function. **C3 15**

exponential function A function with domain $\mathbb{R}$ and rule of the form $f(x) = a^x$ for some positive real number a. The number a is called the base of the exponential function. The most important exponential function is $f(x) = e^x$, where $e = 2.718\,281\ldots$. The function $f(x) = e^x$ is also written as $\exp(x)$. 30 **A3 32**

exponential model (continuous) A model based on a first-order differential equation of the form $dy/dx = Ky$, where K is a constant. Continuous exponential models can be used to model population variation and radioactive decay. 43 **C3 32**

exponential model (discrete) A model for population variation, based on the assumption of a constant proportionate growth rate, r. The model is described by the recurrence relation $P_{n+1} = (1 + r)P_n$, where P_n is the population at n years after some chosen starting time. 31 **B1 22**

finite decimal A number whose decimal representation has a finite number of decimal places. **A0 23**

finite geometric series A sum of the form $a + ar + ar^2 + \cdots + ar^n$. 27 **A1 28**

finite sequence A sequence with a finite number of terms. **A1 6**

first-order differential equation A differential equation that involves the first derivative, dy/dx say, and no higher derivatives. 42 **C3 6**

fit value The predicted value of an observation or measurement, based on a model fitted to data. It is the value of the dependent variable which, according to the model, corresponds to a given value of the explanatory variable. 48 **D4 33**

force A push or pull which, if not counteracted, causes the acceleration of an object. **B3 39**

force diagram A diagrammatic representation of the forces acting on an object. **B3 41**

frequency diagram A diagram that represents a data set in which each value (or group of values) is represented by a rectangle whose height is equal to the frequency of that value (or group of values). **D1 35**

frequency (of a particular value, or of an event) The number of times that the value, or event, occurs. **D2 21**

function A (real) function consists of a subset of $\mathbb{R}$, called the domain, and a rule that associates with each x in the domain a unique y in $\mathbb{R}$. A function may also be referred to as a *mapping* or a *transformation*. 28 **A3 6**

general solution (of a differential equation) The set of all possible solutions of the differential equation, usually involving one or more arbitrary constants. 42 **C3 9**

geometric distribution The distribution of the number of trials needed to obtain a success in a sequence of trials of an experiment in which the probability of success in each trial is the same. The probabilities of obtaining the values $1, 2, 3, \ldots$ form a geometric sequence. 45 **D1 39**

geometric form (of a vector) The description of a vector $\mathbf{a}$ in terms of its magnitude $|\mathbf{a}|$ and its direction θ. 36 **B3 11**

geometric mean The geometric mean of a set of n positive numbers is the nth root of the product of the numbers. **A1 19**

geometric sequence A sequence in which each term (apart from the first) is obtained by multiplying the previous term by a fixed number. 26 **A1 19**

geometric series See *finite geometric series* and *infinite geometric series*.

gradient (of a graph at a point) The gradient of the tangent to the graph at the point. **C1 7**

gradient (of a line) See *slope (of a line)*.

graph (of a real function f) The set of points $(x, f(x))$ in the Cartesian plane. **A3 9**

half-life The time that it takes for the mass of a radioactive substance to decay to half of its original amount. 43 **C3 28**

histogram A diagram that represents a data set in which each value (or group of values) is represented by a rectangle whose area is proportional to the frequency of that value (or group of values). **D2 15**

hypotenuse The longest side of a right-angled triangle. **A2 21**

i-component (of a vector a) The number a_1 in the component form of the vector $\mathbf{a} = a_1\mathbf{i} + a_2\mathbf{j}$. 36 **B3 16**

identity matrix A square matrix with all the elements on its leading diagonal equal to 1 and all the other elements equal to 0. 35 **B2 35**

image (of x under f) The output of the function f for a given input x, that is, the value of $f(x)$. 28 **A3 7**

image set The complete set of output values of a function. 28 **A3 12**

implicit differentiation The process of using the Chain Rule to differentiate a function such as $z = H(y)$, where y is a function of x, with respect to x. 43 **C3 16**

implicit solution (of a differential equation) A solution of the form $H(y) = F(x)$, where H and F are known functions, and $H(y) \neq y$. **C3 15**

increasing function A real function f with the property that for all x_1, x_2 in the domain of f, if $x_1 < x_2$, then $f(x_1) < f(x_2)$. 29 **A3 36**

increasing on an interval A function f is increasing on an interval I if, for all x_1, x_2 in I, if $x_1 < x_2$, then $f(x_1) < f(x_2)$. 39 **C1 23**

indefinite integral (of a function $f(x)$) The expression $F(x) + c$, where $F(x)$ is an integral of $f(x)$ and c is an arbitrary constant. 40 **C2 8**

independent events Two events are independent if the occurrence (or not) of one event is not influenced by whether or not the other occurs. 45 **D1 29**

independent variable A variable that can take any value appropriate to the problem; that is, its value does not depend on the value of any other variable. **A0 28**

infinite decimal A number whose decimal representation has infinitely many decimal places. **A0 23**

infinite geometric series A sum of the form $a + ar + ar^2 + \cdots$. 31 **B1 48**

infinite sequence A sequence that has a first term but no final term. **A1 6**

initial condition (for a first-order differential equation) A condition requiring that the dependent variable take a specified value when the independent variable has a given value. 42 **C3 10**

initial-value problem The combination of a first-order differential equation and an initial condition. 42 **C3 10**

integers The positive and negative whole numbers, together with zero: $\ldots, -3, -2, -1, 0, 1, 2, 3, \ldots$. **A0 23**

integral (of a function f) A function F for which $F' = f$. 40 **C2 7**

integrand In an integral, the function which is to be integrated. 40 **C2 8**

integration The process of finding either an integral or the indefinite integral of a function. 40 **C2 8**

intercept A value of x or y where a line (or curve) meets the x-axis or y-axis, respectively. The x-intercept is the value of x where it meets the x-axis. The y-intercept is the value of y where it meets the y-axis. 29 **A2 11**

interquartile range The difference between the upper quartile and the lower quartile of a batch of data. 47 **D4 11**

interval An unbroken subset of the real line. **A3 7**

inverse function The inverse function f^{-1} of a one-one function f reverses the effect of f; that is, if $f(x) = y$, then $f^{-1}(y) = x$. The domain of f^{-1} is the image set of f. 29 **A3 37**

inverse of a matrix If two square matrices $\mathbf{A}$ and $\mathbf{B}$ have the property that $\mathbf{AB} = \mathbf{BA} = \mathbf{I}$, where $\mathbf{I}$ is the identity matrix, then each of $\mathbf{A}$ and $\mathbf{B}$ is the inverse of the other. 35 **B2 36**

invertible matrix A square matrix that has a non-zero determinant, and therefore has an inverse. 35 **B2 38**

irrational number A real number that is not rational, and hence is a non-recurring decimal. **A0 24**

j-component (of a vector a) The number a_2 in the component form of the vector $\mathbf{a} = a_1\mathbf{i} + a_2\mathbf{j}$. 36 **B3 16**

leading diagonal (of a matrix) The diagonal of a square matrix which starts at the top left and ends at the bottom right of the matrix. **B2 36**

least squares A method for fitting a line or curve to a set of data points in such a way that the sum of the squared residuals is as small as possible. 48 **D4 34**

least squares fit line The straight line fitted using the method of least squares. 48 **D4 35**

left-skew See *skewed.*

limit (of a sequence) The value near which a convergent sequence settles in the long term. 32 **B1 42**

limits of integration The numbers a and b in the expression $\int_a^b f(x)\,dx$. The number a is the lower limit and b is the upper limit. 40 **C2 41**

linear expression A sum consisting of first powers of the variables and a constant. **A0 35**

linear function A real function with rule of the form $f(x) = mx + c$, for some constants m and c. **A3 9**

linear recurrence sequence A recurrence sequence with recurrence relation of the form $x_{n+1} = rx_n + d$, where r and d are constants. 26 **A1 24**

local maximum A stationary point at $x = x_0$ of a function $f(x)$ for which $f(x_0)$ is greater than any other function value in the immediate vicinity of x_0. 39 **C1 22**

local minimum A stationary point at $x = x_0$ of a function $f(x)$ for which $f(x_0)$ is less than any other function value in the immediate vicinity of x_0. 39 **C1 22**

locus A curve defined by a particular property. **A2 7**

logarithm to the base a The inverse function of the exponential function $f(x) = a^x$, where $a > 0$ and $a \neq 1$. The logarithm function is written $\log_a$ and has domain $(0, \infty)$. 30 **A3 42**

logistic model A model for population variation, based on the assumption of a proportionate growth rate of the form $R(P) = r(1 - P/E)$, where r and E are positive parameters. 31 **B1 29**

logistic recurrence relation A recurrence relation of the form $P_{n+1} - P_n = rP_n(1 - P_n/E)$, where r and E are positive parameters. 31 **B1 29**

log-linear plot A plot of the natural logarithm of the dependent variable against the independent variable. 43 **C3 33**

long-term behaviour of a sequence The way in which the sequence develops as more and more terms are considered. 26 **A1 32**

lower quartile See *quartiles*.

magnitude (of a real number) See *modulus (of a real number x)*.

magnitude (of a vector a) The length of an arrow representing the vector; it is written as $|\mathbf{a}|$. 36 **B3 10**

main diagonal (of a matrix) See *leading diagonal (of a matrix)*.

many-one function A function that is not one-one. **A3 36**

mapping See *function*.

mass A measure of the amount of matter that an object contains. **B3 40**

mathematical model A collection of formulas that attempts to quantify how some aspect of the real world behaves. 4 **A1 36**

matrix A rectangular array of numbers. Each number in a matrix is called an element of the matrix. A row of the matrix is a horizontal line of numbers in the array, and a column of the matrix is a vertical line of numbers in the array. A matrix that has m rows and n columns is called an $m \times n$ matrix. Matrices of appropriate sizes can be added, subtracted and multiplied. 33 **B2 11**

matrix–vector multiplication The process of multiplying a vector by a matrix. 33 **B2 13**

mean An average of a finite set of numbers. See *arithmetic mean, geometric mean.*

mean (of a probability distribution, or of a random variable) The average value predicted by the probability model. 45 **D1 43**

median If the values in a batch of data are written in order of increasing size, then the median is the middle value when the batch size is odd, or the average of the middle two values when the batch size is even. 47 **D4 8**

mode A peak in a distribution. A distribution that has only one peak is called unimodal; a distribution that has two peaks is called bimodal. **D2 9**

modelling cycle The process of choosing a (mathematical) model, trying it out, evaluating it, and possibly changing it. 4 **A1 37**

modulus (of a real number x) The magnitude of x, regardless of its sign; it is written as $|x|$. 28 **A3 13**

natural logarithm The logarithm function with base e, where $e = 2.718\,281\ldots$; it is often written as ln. 30 **A3 45**

natural numbers The positive integers: $1, 2, 3, \ldots$. **A0 23**

network diagram A mathematical representation of a physical network. Each point at which a network branches is called a node, and two nodes of a network may be connected by a pipe. 33 **B2 6**

newton The SI unit of force. **B3 40**

node (of a network) See *network diagram*.

non-invertible matrix A square matrix that has zero determinant, and therefore has no inverse. 35 **B2 38**

normal curve The graph of the probability density function of a normal distribution. 46 **D2 13**

normal distribution A particular model for the variation in a continuous random variable. 46 **D2 13**

normal reaction The force acting on an object due to contact with a surface, which is directed at right angles to that surface. **B3 41**

nth root of a The non-negative number which, when raised to the power n, gives the answer a. 23 **A0 26**

null hypothesis A hypothesis about a population (or populations) which may or may not be rejected as the result of a hypothesis test. 48 **D4 18**

one-one function A function f with the property that for all x_1, x_2 in the domain of f, if $x_1 \neq x_2$, then $f(x_1) \neq f(x_2)$. 29 **A3 36**

optimisation The process of finding optimum values of a function on an interval. 40 **C1 32**

optimum values (on an interval) The greatest or least values attained by a function on the interval. 40 **C1 32**

order (of a differential equation) The order of the highest derivative that appears in the differential equation. **C3 6**

parabola The graph of a quadratic function. **A3 19**

Parallelogram Rule A rule for the addition of two vectors that are in geometric form. 36 **B3 14**

parameter (1) A variable used when defining a family of mathematical objects, such as a recurrence system. 26 **A1 14**

parameter (2) A variable, often t, used when defining a curve in terms of the motion of a point along the curve. 28 **A2 40**

parametrisation (of a curve) The process of describing the coordinates of points on the curve in terms of a parameter. 28 **A2 40**

particle A material object whose size and internal structure may be neglected (for modelling purposes). **B3 40**

particular solution (of a differential equation) A single solution of the differential equation, which contains no arbitrary constant. 42 **C3 9**

periodic function A function f whose graph is unchanged by a horizontal translation through the period p; that is, $f(x+p) = f(x)$ for all x in the domain. **A3 28**

perpendicular bisector (of a line segment AB) The line that cuts AB halfway along its length and is at right angles to AB. **A2 24**

pipe (of a network) See *network diagram*.

polar coordinates (of a point A) The numbers r and θ for the point A with Cartesian coordinates $(r\cos\theta, r\sin\theta)$. **B3 19**

polynomial A polynomial (of degree n) is an expression of the form $a_n x^n + a_{n-1}x^{n-1} + \cdots + a_1 x + a_0$, where $a_n \neq 0$. **A3 47**

polynomial function A function whose rule is a polynomial; for example, a quadratic function. **A3 47**

population The collection of all the individual values or members of a specified group of interest. **D2 8**

population mean The mean of all the values in a population or, when a probability distribution is used to model the variation in the population, the mean of this probability distribution. 46 **D2 23**

population parameter A summary measure for a population. The population mean μ and the population standard deviation σ are examples of population parameters. 46 **D2 20**

population standard deviation The square root of the population variance. 46 **D2 24**

population variance The mean squared deviation of the values in a population from the population mean. **D2 24**

position The position of a particle, with respect to a chosen axis, is a measure of how far it is from the origin and of its direction relative to the origin. 41 **C2 26**

position vector A displacement vector whose arrow has its tail at the origin. **B3 12**

power function A function with rule of the form $f(x) = x^n$, where n is any real number. **C1 16**

power (of a square matrix) The nth power of a square matrix $\mathbf{A}$, written $\mathbf{A}^n$, is obtained by repeated matrix multiplication. 33 **B2 21**

predicted value See *fit value*.

probability density function If a curve is used to model the variation in a population, and the total area between the curve and the x-axis is 1, then the function that defines the curve is a probability density function. According to this model, the proportion of the population between two values a and b ($a < b$) is given by the area under the curve between $x = a$ and $x = b$. 45 **D2 13**

probability distribution The probability distribution of a random variable gives the probabilities of all the possible values that the random variable can take. 45 **D1 38**

probability function The probability function of a discrete random variable X is a function that gives, for each value j, the value of the probability $P(X = j)$. 45 **D1 37**

probability (of an event) The long-run proportion of occasions on which the event occurs.	45	**D1 10**
product matrix The result of multiplying two matrices together.		**B2 16**
proportionate growth rate The proportionate birth rate minus the proportionate death rate for a population.		**B1 22**
proportionate growth rate (continuous exponential model) The constant K in the differential equation $dP/dt = KP$, used to model population variation.	43	**C3 31**
quadratic expression An expression in the form $ax^2 + bx + c$, where $a \neq 0$.		**A0 37**
quartic function A polynomial function of degree 4.		**C1 20**
quartiles The median and quartiles of a batch of data divide the batch into four roughly equal parts. Roughly 25% of the values in the batch are smaller than the lower quartile, and roughly 25% of the values are greater than the upper quartile. When the values are written in order of increasing size, the lower quartile is the median of the values to the left of the median, and the upper quartile is the median of the values to the right of the median.	47	**D4 8**
radius (of a circle) The distance from the centre of a circle to any point on the circumference of the circle.		**A2 20**
random variable A quantity that can take different values on different occasions.		**D1 36**
range The range of a batch of data is the difference between the maximum and minimum values.	47	**D4 11**
rational number A real number that can be represented as a fraction, and hence as a recurring decimal.		**A0 23**
real function A function for which both the inputs and the outputs are real numbers.		**A3 9**
real line A number line that includes all real numbers.		**A0 24**
real number A number that can be represented as a decimal.		**A0 23**
reciprocal function The function whose rule is $f(x) = 1/x$.		**A3 10**
recurrence relation A formula that defines each term of a sequence by referring to a previous term or terms of the sequence.	26	**A1 11**
recurrence system The specification of a sequence by an initial term or terms, a recurrence relation and a subscript range.	26	**A1 11**
regression line The regression line of y on x is another name for the least squares fit line. See also *least squares fit line*.	48	**D4 35**
residual When a line is fitted to a set of data points, the residual of each data pair may be calculated using the relationship RESIDUAL = DATA − FIT, where DATA is the y-coordinate of the data pair and FIT is the y-value predicted by the line for the corresponding x-coordinate.	48	**D4 33**
resultant The sum of two vectors.		**B3 13**
right-skew See *skewed*.		

rise from A to B The rise from a point $A(x_1, y_1)$ to a point $B(x_2, y_2)$ is $y_2 - y_1$.		**A2**	**9**
root (of an equation) An alternative term for a *solution of an equation*.			
row (of a matrix) See *matrix*.			
rule (of a function) The process for converting each input value in the domain of the function into a unique output value. See *function*.	28	**A3**	**6**
run from A to B The run from a point $A(x_1, y_1)$ to a point $B(x_2, y_2)$ is $x_2 - x_1$.		**A2**	**9**
sample A subset of a population.	46	**D2**	**8**
sample mean The mean $\overline{x}$ of a sample.	46	**D2**	**21**
sample standard deviation The sample standard deviation s is the square root of the sample variance.	46	**D2**	**25**
sample variance The mean squared deviation, from the sample mean, of the values in a sample.		**D2**	**25**
sampling distribution of the mean The distribution of the means of all possible samples of size n from a population is called the sampling distribution of the mean for samples of size n.	47	**D3**	**10**
sampling error An error due to the selection of an unrepresentative sample.		**D3**	**30**
scalar A real number.		**B2**	**23**
scalar multiplication (of a matrix) The operation of multiplying each element of a matrix $\mathbf{A}$ by a real number k. The resulting matrix $k\mathbf{A}$ is called the scalar multiple of $\mathbf{A}$ by the real number k.	33	**B2**	**23**
scaling (of a graph) Squashing or stretching the graph in the x-direction or y-direction.	29	**A3**	**21**
secant (of an angle θ) The secant of θ is $1/\cos\theta$, provided that $\cos\theta \neq 0$.		**A2**	**36**
second derivative (of a function f at a point) The value of the second derived function f'' at the point.	40	**C1**	**28**
second derived function (of a function f) The function f'' defined by the process of differentiating the derived function f' of f.	40	**C1**	**28**
separable differential equation A differential equation of the form $dy/dx = f(x)g(y)$.	43	**C3**	**19**
separation of variables A method for solving separable differential equations.	43	**C3**	**19**
sequence An ordered list (finite or infinite) of numbers, called the terms of the sequence.	26	**A1**	**6**
series A sum of consecutive terms of a sequence.	31	**B1**	**11**
sigma notation A concise way of expressing finite and infinite series.	31	**B1**	**11**
significance level The significance level of a test is the probability (often written as a percentage) that the null hypothesis is wrongly rejected.	48	**D4**	**23**

sine (of an angle θ) The second coordinate of the point P on the circumference of the unit circle, centre O, where the angle between the positive x-axis and the line segment OP is θ. By convention, angles are measured positively in an anticlockwise direction from the positive x-axis. 27 **A2 33**

Sine Rule A rule that relates pairs of sides and the corresponding opposite angles of a triangle. 37 **B3 31**

size (of a matrix) An $m \times n$ matrix has size $m \times n$. 33 **B2 18**

skewed A data set which is not symmetric (or, equivalently, for which a frequency diagram is not symmetric) is said to be skewed. If the large data values are more spread out than the small data values, so that a frequency diagram has a longer right tail than left tail, then the data set is right-skew. If the left tail of a frequency diagram is longer than the right tail, then the data set is left-skew. The terms right-skew and left-skew are also used to describe probability distributions. **D2 11**

slope (of a line) If A and B are two points on a line, then the slope of the line is (rise from A to B) $\div$ (run from A to B). The slope is also called the gradient. 27 **A2 9**

smooth A function f is said to be smooth if the derivative exists at each point of the domain of f. **C1 14**

solution of a differential equation A function, $y = F(x)$ say, (or a more general equation relating the independent and dependent variables) for which the differential equation is satisfied. 42 **C3 6**

solution (of an equation) A value of the unknown for which the equation is satisfied. **A0 35**

solving a triangle The process of determining all the angles and side lengths of a triangle. **A2 37**

speed A (scalar) measure of how fast an object is moving, irrespective of its direction of motion. The speed is the magnitude of the velocity vector. **B3 26**

square matrix A matrix with the same number of rows and columns. **B2 21**

standard error The standard deviation of a sampling distribution. **D3 14** **D4 20**

standard error of the mean The standard deviation of the sampling distribution of the mean for samples of size n, for any given sample size n. 47 **D3 14**

standard normal distribution The normal distribution with mean 0 and standard deviation 1. 46 **D2 36**

stationary point A point x_0 in the domain of a smooth function f at which $f'(x_0) = 0$, or the corresponding point $(x_0, f(x_0))$ on the graph of f. 39 **C1 22**

step size The value of the variable h in Euler's method, which determines the distance between the successive values of x at which solution estimates are calculated. 44 **C3 39**

subscript In the notation a_n, n is called the subscript of a. **A1 7**

subtended angle (at a point)	The angle that lies between two lines drawn from the point to the endpoints of a line segment or an arc of a circle.		**A2 21**
tangent (of an angle θ)	$\tan\theta = \dfrac{\sin\theta}{\cos\theta}$, where $\theta \neq \pm\frac{1}{2}\pi, \pm\frac{3}{2}\pi, \ldots$.	27	**A2 36**
tangent (to a circle)	A line that intersects the circle in precisely one point.		**A2 29**
tangent (to a graph at a point)	The unique line that just 'touches' the graph at the point; that is, the line that most closely approximates the graph near the point.		**C1 7**
tends to infinity (or minus infinity)	The terms of a sequence become arbitrarily large and positive (or arbitrarily large and negative).		**A1 33**
tends to ℓ	The terms of a sequence become arbitrarily close to ℓ.		**A1 33**
tension	The force provided by a taut string (rope, etc.).		**B3 41**
term (of a sequence)	An item of a sequence.	26	**A1 6**
test statistic	A measure calculated from data, which can be used to decide whether or not to reject the null hypothesis.	48	**D4 22**
transformation	See *function*.		
translation (of a graph)	Shifting the graph horizontally or vertically.	29	**A3 20**
triangle of forces	A triangle of arrows which is a geometric representation of the Equilibrium Condition for three forces.		**B3 44**
Triangle Rule	A rule for the addition of two vectors that are in geometric form.	36	**B3 13**
unbounded sequence	A sequence that has terms of arbitrarily large value, either positive or negative.	26	**A1 34**
unimodal	See *mode*.		
unit circle	The circle with radius 1 and centre at the origin.		**A2 33**
upper quartile	See *quartiles*.		
variable	A symbol used to represent a quantity that can vary.		**A0 28**
vector	A matrix consisting of a single column. Each number appearing in the column is called a component of the vector.	33	**B2 10**
velocity (vector)	The rate of change of position of an object. Velocity is a measure of how fast the object is moving and its direction of motion.		**B3 26**
weight	The force on an object due to gravity.		**B3 40**
zero vector	The vector in which every component is 0, denoted by $\mathbf{0}$.		**B3 8**

Background material for MST121

Rounding numbers

To **round** to a given number of **decimal places**, look at the digit one place to the right of the number of places specified. If this digit is 5 or more, then round up; if it is less than 5, then round down.

To **round** to a given number of **significant figures**, start counting significant figures from the first non-zero digit on the left, and follow the rules for rounding.

Scientific notation

In scientific notation, positive numbers are expressed in the form $a \times 10^n$, where a is between 1 and 10, and n is an integer.

Rules for powers

$a^p \times a^q = a^{p+q}$	$a^p \div a^q = a^{p-q}$	$(a^p)^q = a^{pq}$	$a^p b^p = (ab)^p$
$a^{-n} = \dfrac{1}{a^n}$	$a^0 = 1$	$a^{1/n} = \sqrt[n]{a}$	$a^{m/n} = \sqrt[n]{a^m} = (\sqrt[n]{a})^m$

Surds

An irrational number is in **surd** form if it is written in terms of roots of rational numbers. For example, $\sqrt{2}$, $\sqrt[4]{5}$ and $\sqrt[3]{7} + \sqrt[4]{3}$ are numbers in surd form.

Calculating means

To calculate the **mean** of a batch of data, add together the values (x) in the batch to give $\sum x$, and divide by n, the number of values in the batch.

Algebra

Difference of two squares: $a^2 - b^2 = (a-b)(a+b)$.

Squaring a bracket: $(a+b)^2 = a^2 + 2ab + b^2$.

The **solutions of the quadratic equation** $ax^2 + bx + c = 0$, where $a \neq 0$, are

$$x = \frac{-b \pm \sqrt{b^2 - 4ac}}{2a}.$$

To solve two simultaneous linear equations by **substitution**.

1. Rearrange one of the equations so that one unknown is equal to an expression involving the other unknown.
2. Substitute this expression in the other equation.
3. Solve the resulting linear equation for the other unknown.
4. Substitute this solution into either of the original equations to find the remaining unknown.

To solve two simultaneous linear equations by **elimination**.

1. Multiply the two equations by numbers chosen so that one of the unknowns has the same coefficient, possibly with the opposite sign, in both equations.
2. Subtract or add the new equations to eliminate that unknown.
3. Solve the resulting linear equation for the other unknown.
4. Substitute this solution into either of the original equations to find the remaining unknown.

Equivalent rearrangements of inequalities

If the sides of an inequality are interchanged, then the direction of the inequality sign is reversed: $>$ becomes $<$, $\geq$ becomes $\leq$, and vice versa.

The same number can be added to (or subtracted from) both sides of an inequality: if $a < b$, then $a + c < b + c$.

Both sides of an inequality can be multiplied (or divided) by the same positive number: if $a < b$ and $c > 0$, then $ac < bc$.

If both sides of an inequality are multiplied (or divided) by the same negative number, then the direction of the inequality sign changes: if $a < b$ and $c < 0$, then $ac > bc$.

Angle measurement

The angle subtended at the centre of a circle by an arc equal in length to the radius of the circle is defined to be one **radian**. Thus 2π radians $= 360°$, and the rules for converting between degrees and radians are

$$x \text{ radians} = x \times \frac{180}{\pi} \text{ degrees}, \quad y \text{ degrees} = y \times \frac{\pi}{180} \text{ radians}.$$

Polygons

A plane figure which is a closed shape whose sides are straight lines is called a **polygon**. A point where two sides meet is called a **vertex**. A polygon with n sides (and hence n vertices) is referred to as an ***n*-gon**.

The angle sum of an n-gon is $(n - 2)180°$, that is, $(n - 2)\pi$ radians.

An n-gon is said to be **regular** if all its sides are equal and all its angles are equal.

Triangles

A **triangle** is a polygon with three sides. Its angle sum is $180°$, that is, π radians. If all three sides are of equal length, then it is an **equilateral triangle** and all three angles are $60°$. If two sides are of equal length, then it is an **isosceles triangle** and the two angles opposite the equal length sides are equal.

The **area of a triangle** is

◇ $\frac{1}{2}ah$, where a is the length of the base and h is the height;

◇ $\frac{1}{2}ab\sin\theta$, where a and b are two side lengths, and θ is the angle between the sides.

Right-angled triangles

Pythagoras' Theorem: For a triangle ABC with side lengths a, b and c (opposite A, B and C, respectively), where the angle at C is a right angle, $c^2 = a^2 + b^2$.

The side opposite the right angle is known as the **hypotenuse**.

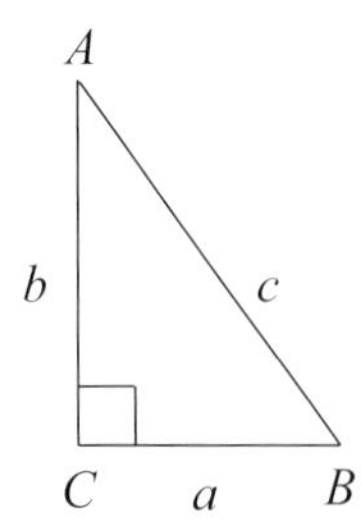

For this triangle, the trigonometric ratios are

$$\sin A = \frac{\text{opposite}}{\text{hypotenuse}} = \frac{a}{c}, \quad \cos A = \frac{\text{adjacent}}{\text{hypotenuse}} = \frac{b}{c}, \quad \tan A = \frac{\text{opposite}}{\text{adjacent}} = \frac{a}{b},$$

$$\operatorname{cosec} A = \frac{\text{hypotenuse}}{\text{opposite}} = \frac{c}{a}, \quad \sec A = \frac{\text{hypotenuse}}{\text{adjacent}} = \frac{c}{b}, \quad \cot A = \frac{\text{adjacent}}{\text{opposite}} = \frac{b}{a}.$$

It follows from Pythagoras' Theorem that $\sin^2 A + \cos^2 A = 1$.

Useful trigonometic ratios

Angle θ in radians	0	$\frac{1}{6}\pi$	$\frac{1}{4}\pi$	$\frac{1}{3}\pi$	$\frac{1}{2}\pi$
Angle θ in degrees	0	30	45	60	90
$\sin\theta$	0	$\frac{1}{2}$	$1/\sqrt{2}$	$\sqrt{3}/2$	1
$\cos\theta$	1	$\sqrt{3}/2$	$1/\sqrt{2}$	$\frac{1}{2}$	0
$\tan\theta$	0	$1/\sqrt{3}$	1	$\sqrt{3}$	Undefined

Sine positive	All positive
Tangent positive	Cosine positive

Quadrilaterals

A **quadrilateral** is a polygon with four sides. Its angle sum is $360°$, that is, 2π radians.

- ◇ A quadrilateral in which opposite sides are equal is a **parallelogram**.
- ◇ A quadrilateral in which all sides are equal is a **rhombus**.
- ◇ A quadrilateral in which all angles are equal (to $90°$) is a **rectangle**.
- ◇ A quadrilateral in which all sides and all angles are equal is a **square**.

In a parallelogram, opposite angles are equal and the two diagonals bisect each other. In a rhombus, the diagonals bisect each other at an angle of $90°$.

The area of a rectangle is $A = lb$, where l is the length and b is the breadth.

Circles

A circle of radius r has

- ◇ circumference $C = 2\pi r = \pi d$, where d is the diameter;
- ◇ area $A = \pi r^2$.

Congruence

Two figures are **congruent** if they have the same shape and the same size.

Two n-gons are congruent if all corresponding sides and angles are equal.

Similarity

Two figures are **similar** if they have the same shape; their sizes need not be the same.

Two n-gons are similar if each angle in one n-gon is equal to the corresponding angle in the other. In this case, the length of each side in one n-gon is the same multiple of the corresponding length in the other.

Prisms

A **prism** is a solid with constant cross-section. A **cylinder** is a prism with circular cross-section.

The surface area of a prism is the sum of the areas of its faces. In particular, the surface area of a cylinder is $A = 2\pi r^2 + 2\pi rh$, where r is the radius of the circular cross-section and h is the length.

The volume of a prism is the area of its cross-section multiplied by its length. In particular, the volume of a cylinder is $V = \pi r^2 h$.

Definitions and results in MST121

The following definitions and results have been collected from the chapters of MST121. They are listed in chapter order. If you cannot find the information you want here, then try the alphabetical listing in the Glossary.

MST121 Chapter A1 Sequences

Types of sequences

Convention: The first term of a sequence has subscript 1, unless otherwise indicated.

An **arithmetic sequence** with first term a and common difference d can be specified by either of the following recurrence systems:

◇ $$x_1 = a, \quad x_{n+1} = x_n + d \quad (n = 1, 2, 3, \ldots),$$

with closed form $x_n = a + (n-1)d$ $(n = 1, 2, 3, \ldots)$;

◇ $$x_0 = a, \quad x_{n+1} = x_n + d \quad (n = 0, 1, 2, \ldots),$$

with closed form $x_n = a + nd$ $(n = 0, 1, 2, \ldots)$.

A **geometric sequence** with first term a and common ratio r can be specified by either of the following recurrence systems:

◇ $$x_1 = a, \quad x_{n+1} = rx_n \quad (n = 1, 2, 3, \ldots),$$

with closed form $x_n = ar^{n-1}$ $(n = 1, 2, 3, \ldots)$;

◇ $$x_0 = a, \quad x_{n+1} = rx_n \quad (n = 0, 1, 2, \ldots),$$

with closed form $x_n = ar^n$ $(n = 0, 1, 2, \ldots)$.

A **linear recurrence sequence** with parameters a, r and d can be specified by either of the following recurrence systems:

◇ $$x_1 = a, \quad x_{n+1} = rx_n + d \quad (n = 1, 2, 3, \ldots),$$

with closed form (when $r \neq 1$)

$$x_n = \left(a + \frac{d}{r-1}\right) r^{n-1} - \frac{d}{r-1} \quad (n = 1, 2, 3, \ldots);$$

◇ $$x_0 = a, \quad x_{n+1} = rx_n + d \quad (n = 0, 1, 2, \ldots),$$

with closed form (when $r \neq 1$)

$$x_n = \left(a + \frac{d}{r-1}\right) r^{n} - \frac{d}{r-1} \quad (n = 0, 1, 2, \ldots).$$

Long-term behaviour of sequences

Range of r	Behaviour of r^n
$r > 1$	$r^n \to \infty$ as $n \to \infty$
$r = 1$	Remains constant: $1, 1, 1, \ldots$
$0 < r < 1$	$r^n \to 0$ as $n \to \infty$
$r = 0$	Remains constant: $0, 0, 0, \ldots$
$-1 < r < 0$	$r^n \to 0$ as $n \to \infty$, alternates in sign
$r = -1$	Alternates between -1 and $+1$
$r < -1$	r^n is unbounded, alternates in sign

Sum of a finite geometric series

The sum of a finite geometric series with first term a and common ratio r ($r \neq 1$) is

$$a + ar + ar^2 + \cdots + ar^n = a\left(\frac{1 - r^{n+1}}{1 - r}\right).$$

MST121 Chapter A2 Lines and circles

Lines

Type	Slope	Equation
Parallel to x-axis	$m = 0$	$y = c$, where c is a constant
Parallel to y-axis	Infinite	$x = d$, where d is a constant
Not parallel to y-axis	$m = (y_2 - y_1)/(x_2 - x_1)$, where (x_1, y_1) and (x_2, y_2) are points on the line	$y - y_1 = m(x - x_1)$ or $y = mx + c$, where c is the y-intercept

If two lines are **parallel**, then they have equal slopes. If two lines are **perpendicular**, then either the product of their slopes is -1 or one has slope 0 and the other has infinite slope.

The **distance** between two points (x_1, y_1) and (x_2, y_2) is

$$\sqrt{(x_2 - x_1)^2 + (y_2 - y_1)^2}.$$

The **midpoint** of a line segment with endpoints (x_1, y_1) and (x_2, y_2) is

$$\left(\frac{x_1 + x_2}{2}, \frac{y_1 + y_2}{2}\right).$$

Circles

Geometrically, a **circle** is the set of points that are at a fixed distance (the radius) from a specified point (the centre). Algebraically, a circle with centre (a, b) and radius r has the equation

$$(x - a)^2 + (y - b)^2 = r^2.$$

To find the equation of a circle, given three points A, B and C on the circle, find the perpendicular bisectors of the line segments AB and BC. The centre of the circle is the intersection point of the two perpendicular bisectors. The radius of the circle is the distance from the centre to any of the points A, B or C.

To **complete the square** of $x^2 + 2px$, use

$$x^2 + 2px = x^2 + 2px + p^2 - p^2 = (x + p)^2 - p^2.$$

Trigonometry

Let $P(x, y)$ be a point on the unit circle (with centre O) such that the angle from the positive x-axis to OP is θ (measured anticlockwise if θ is positive, clockwise if θ is negative). Then

$$\cos\theta = x, \qquad \sin\theta = y \quad \text{and} \quad \tan\theta = \frac{\sin\theta}{\cos\theta} \quad (\text{provided that } \cos\theta \neq 0).$$

Trigonometric identities

$\cos(-\theta) = \cos\theta$	$\cos(\pi - \theta) = -\cos\theta$	$\cos(\theta + 2\pi) = \cos\theta$
$\sin(-\theta) = -\sin\theta$	$\sin(\pi - \theta) = \sin\theta$	$\sin(\theta + 2\pi) = \sin\theta$
$\tan(-\theta) = -\tan\theta$	$\tan(\pi - \theta) = -\tan\theta$	$\tan(\theta + \pi) = \tan\theta$
$\cos(\frac{1}{2}\pi - \theta) = \sin\theta$	$\sin(\frac{1}{2}\pi - \theta) = \cos\theta$	$\cos^2\theta + \sin^2\theta = 1$

Parametrisation of lines and circles

◇ A line with slope m passing through the point (x_1, y_1) has parametric equations

$$x = t + x_1, \quad y = mt + y_1.$$

◇ A line passing through the two points (x_1, y_1) and (x_2, y_2) has parametric equations

$$x = x_1 + t(x_2 - x_1), \quad y = y_1 + t(y_2 - y_1).$$

◇ A circle with centre at (a, b) and radius r has parametric equations

$$x = a + r\cos\theta, \quad y = b + r\sin\theta \quad (0 \le \theta \le 2\pi).$$

MST121 Chapter A3 Functions

Functions

A (**real**) **function** is specified by giving

◇ the **domain**, that is, the set of allowable input values, which are real numbers;

◇ the **rule** for converting each input value to a unique output value, which is also a real number.

The output of a function f for a given input x is called the **image** of x under f, and is written $f(x)$. The set of all outputs of the function f is called the **image set** of f.

Convention: When a function is specified just by a rule, it is understood that the domain of the function is the largest possible set of real numbers for which the rule is applicable.

Function notation

A standard notation used to specify a function f is

$$f(x) = x^2 + 1 \quad (0 \le x \le 6).$$

Other notations used to specify the same function f are

◇ $f : x \longmapsto x^2 + 1 \quad (0 \le x \le 6)$;

◇ $f : [0, 6] \longrightarrow \mathbb{R}$
$\quad x \longmapsto x^2 + 1.$

Modulus of a real number

The **modulus**, or **absolute value**, of a real number x is the magnitude of x, regardless of sign, denoted by $|x|$. Thus

$$|x| = \begin{cases} x, & \text{if } x \ge 0, \\ -x, & \text{if } x < 0. \end{cases}$$

Translating and scaling a known graph

Graph	Translation or scaling of $y = f(x)$
$y = f(x + p)$	Horizontal translation by p units to the left (right if p is negative)
$y = f(x) + q$	Vertical translation by q units upwards (downwards if q is negative)
$y = af(x)$	y-scaling with factor a
$y = f(bx)$	x-scaling with factor $1/b$

The scalings and translations in the table above can, with two exceptions, be applied in any order with the same result. The exceptions are that the result of applying both a horizontal translation and an x-scaling depends in general on the order in which these are applied, and similarly for both a vertical translation and a y-scaling.

Graphing quadratic functions

To sketch the graph of a quadratic function $f(x) = ax^2 + bx + c$, first write the function in completed-square form: $f(x) = a(x + p)^2 + q$. Then start with the graph of $y = x^2$ and perform

1. a y-scaling with factor a;
2. a horizontal translation by p units to the left (right if p is negative);
3. a vertical translation by q units upwards (downwards if q is negative).

The graph is a parabola with vertex $(-p, q)$, which is the lowest point if $a > 0$ and the highest point if $a < 0$. Its axis of symmetry is $x = -p$.

The y-intercept is found by setting $x = 0$ to give $f(0) = c$. The x-intercepts (if any) are found by setting $y = 0$ and solving $ax^2 + bx + c = 0$.

Inverse functions

A real function f is **one-one** if it has the following property: for all x_1, x_2 in the domain of f, if $x_1 \neq x_2$, then $f(x_1) \neq f(x_2)$.

A real function f is **increasing** if it has the following property: for all x_1, x_2 in the domain of f, if $x_1 < x_2$, then $f(x_1) < f(x_2)$.

A real function f is **decreasing** if it has the following property: for all x_1, x_2 in the domain of f, if $x_1 < x_2$, then $f(x_1) > f(x_2)$.

If a function is increasing (or decreasing), then it is one-one.

When a function f is one-one, an **inverse function** f^{-1} can be defined which reverses the action of f.

◇ To obtain the rule for the function f^{-1} (in terms of x), solve the equation $y = f(x)$ to obtain x in terms of y, and then exchange the roles of x and y. The image set of f is the domain of f^{-1}, and vice versa.

◇ To obtain the graph of $y = f^{-1}(x)$, reflect the graph of $y = f(x)$ in the 45° line.

Inverse trigonometric functions

The function $f(x) = \sin x$ $(-\frac{1}{2}\pi \leq x \leq \frac{1}{2}\pi)$ has an inverse function **arcsine** with domain $[-1, 1]$ and image set $[-\frac{1}{2}\pi, \frac{1}{2}\pi]$. Thus, for $-1 \leq y \leq 1$,

$$x = \arcsin y \quad \text{means that} \quad y = \sin x \text{ and } -\tfrac{1}{2}\pi \leq x \leq \tfrac{1}{2}\pi.$$

The function $f(x) = \cos x$ $(0 \leq x \leq \pi)$ has an inverse function **arccosine** with domain $[-1, 1]$ and image set $[0, \pi]$. Thus, for $-1 \leq y \leq 1$,

$$x = \arccos y \quad \text{means that} \quad y = \cos x \text{ and } 0 \leq x \leq \pi.$$

The function $f(x) = \tan x$ $(-\frac{1}{2}\pi < x < \frac{1}{2}\pi)$ has an inverse function **arctangent** with domain $(-\infty, \infty)$ and image set $(-\frac{1}{2}\pi, \frac{1}{2}\pi)$. Thus, for $-\infty < y < \infty$,

$$x = \arctan y \quad \text{means that} \quad y = \tan x \text{ and } -\tfrac{1}{2}\pi < x < \tfrac{1}{2}\pi.$$

Logarithms

An exponential function $f(x) = a^x$, where $a > 0$ and $a \neq 1$, has domain $\mathbb{R}$ and image set $(0, \infty)$. Its inverse function, called **logarithm** to the **base** a and denoted by $\log_a$, has domain $(0, \infty)$ and image set $\mathbb{R}$. Thus, for $y > 0$,

$$x = \log_a y \quad \text{means that} \quad y = a^x.$$

Combining these results gives

$$x = \log_a(a^x), \quad \text{for } x \text{ in } \mathbb{R}, \quad \text{and} \quad y = a^{\log_a y}, \quad \text{for } y > 0.$$

The **natural logarithm** has base $e = 2.718\,281\ldots$ and is often written as ln. The **common logarithm** has base 10 and is often written as log.

Provided that $a > 0$ and $a \neq 1$, the logarithm to the base a has the following properties:

(a) $\log_a 1 = 0$, $\log_a a = 1$;

(b) for $x > 0$ and $y > 0$,

  (i) $\log_a(xy) = \log_a x + \log_a y$,

  (ii) $\log_a(x/y) = \log_a x - \log_a y$;

(c) for $x > 0$ and p in $\mathbb{R}$, $\quad \log_a(x^p) = p \log_a x$.

To use logarithms to solve an equation of the form $a^x = k$, where $k > 0$ and $a > 0, a \neq 1$, apply the function ln to both sides of the equation, and use property (c) to obtain

$$x = \frac{\ln k}{\ln a}.$$

MST121 Chapter B1 Modelling with sequences

Formulas for sums

$$\sum_{i=1}^{n} c_i = c_1 + c_2 + \cdots + c_n$$

$$\sum_{i=0}^{n} ar^i = a + ar + ar^2 + \cdots + ar^n = a\left(\frac{1-r^{n+1}}{1-r}\right) \quad (r \neq 1)$$

$$\sum_{i=0}^{\infty} ar^i = \frac{a}{1-r} \quad (|r| < 1)$$

$$\sum_{i=1}^{n}(a + bx_i) = an + b\sum_{i=1}^{n} x_i \qquad \sum_{i=m}^{n}(a + bx_i) = a(n-m+1) + b\sum_{i=m}^{n} x_i$$

$$\sum_{i=1}^{n} i = 1 + 2 + 3 + \cdots + n = \tfrac{1}{2}n(n+1)$$

Exponential model

The (discrete) exponential model for population variation is based on the assumption of a constant proportionate growth rate, r. The model is described by either the recurrence relation

$$P_{n+1} = (1+r)P_n \quad (n = 0, 1, 2, \ldots),$$

or its closed-form solution

$$P_n = (1+r)^n P_0 \quad (n = 0, 1, 2, \ldots),$$

where P_n is the population size at n years after some chosen starting time. The proportionate growth rate r is the proportionate birth rate minus the proportionate death rate.

Logistic model

The logistic model for population variation is based on the assumption of a proportionate growth rate $R(P)$ of the form $R(P) = r(1 - P/E)$, where r and E are positive parameters. The model is described by the recurrence relation

$$P_{n+1} - P_n = rP_n\left(1 - \frac{P_n}{E}\right) \quad (n = 0, 1, 2, \ldots),$$

where P_n is the population size at n years after some chosen starting time. The positive constant r represents the proportionate growth rate of the population when the population size is small, and the positive constant E represents the equilibrium population level (the population size at which the proportionate growth rate is zero).

The long-term behaviour of sequences generated by the logistic recurrence relation (with $0 < P_0 \leq E(1 + 1/r)$) depends on the value of r, as shown in the table below.

Range of r	Long-term behaviour of P_n
$0 < r \leq 1$	Settles close to (converges to) E, with values always just below E
$1 < r \leq 2$	Settles close to E, with values alternating between just above and just below E
$2 < r \leq 2.44$	2-cycle, with one value above E and one value below E
$2.45 \leq r \leq 2.54$	4-cycle, with two values above E and two values below E
$2.6 \leq r \leq 3$	Chaotic variation between bounds (with some exceptions)

Convergence and limits

If a sequence P_n settles down in the long term to values that are effectively constant, then P_n is said to be **convergent**. The value near which P_n settles in the long term is called the **limit** of the sequence, written

$$\lim_{n\to\infty} P_n.$$

If a sequence P_n given by a recurrence relation converges, then it converges to the value of a constant sequence that satisfies the recurrence relation. To find such values, substitute $P_n = c$ and $P_{n+1} = c$ into the recurrence relation and solve for c.

Reciprocal Rule

If the terms of a sequence b_n are of the form $1/a_n$, where terms of the sequence a_n become arbitrarily large as n increases, then $\lim\limits_{n\to\infty} b_n = 0$.

Constant Multiple Rule

If the terms of a sequence b_n are of the form ca_n, where $\lim\limits_{n\to\infty} a_n = 0$, and c is a constant, then $\lim\limits_{n\to\infty} b_n = 0$.

Long-term 'basic sequence' behaviour

The long-term behaviour of the sequence r^n $(n = 1, 2, 3, \ldots)$ is as follows.

- If $|r| > 1$, then $|r^n| \to \infty$ as $n \to \infty$. (If $r > 1$, then $r^n \to \infty$ as $n \to \infty$; if $r < -1$, then r^n is unbounded and alternates in sign.)
- If $|r| < 1$, then $r^n \to 0$ as $n \to \infty$.
- If $r = 1$, then $r^n = 1$. If $r = -1$, then r^n alternates between 1 and -1.

The long-term behaviour of the sequence n^p $(n = 1, 2, 3, \ldots)$ is as follows.

- If $p > 0$, then $n^p \to \infty$ as $n \to \infty$.
- If $p < 0$, then $n^p \to 0$ as $n \to \infty$.
- If $p = 0$, then $n^p = 1$.

MST121 Chapter B2 Modelling with matrices

Networks and matrices

A physical network can be represented by a **network diagram** and also by a matrix. The entries of the matrix indicate the proportion of the input flowing through each pipe of the network.

The network diagram and the matrix shown below represent the same physical network having two input nodes A and B, and three output nodes U, V and W.

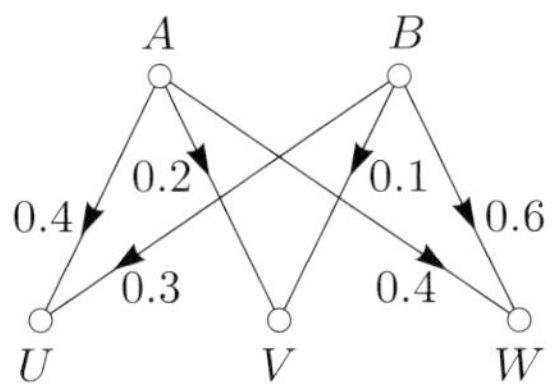

$$\begin{pmatrix} 0.4 & 0.3 \\ 0.2 & 0.1 \\ 0.4 & 0.6 \end{pmatrix}$$

If the outputs of one network feed directly into an equal number of inputs in a second network, then the matrix representing the combined network is obtained by multiplying the matrices representing the two original networks.

Arithmetic of matrices and vectors

A **matrix** is a rectangular array of numbers. Each number in a matrix is called an **element**. A matrix with m rows and n columns is called an $m \times n$ matrix, and has **size** $m \times n$. The element in row i and column j of a matrix $\mathbf{A}$ is written as a_{ij}.

Matrix multiplication

Two matrices $\mathbf{A}$ and $\mathbf{B}$ can be multiplied only if the number of columns of $\mathbf{A}$ equals the number of rows of $\mathbf{B}$. The element in the ith row and jth column of the product matrix $\mathbf{AB}$ is obtained by adding up the products of corresponding elements of the ith row of $\mathbf{A}$ and the jth column of $\mathbf{B}$.

Thus, if $\mathbf{A}$ is an $m \times n$ matrix and $\mathbf{B}$ is an $n \times p$ matrix, then $\mathbf{C} = \mathbf{AB}$ is an $m \times p$ matrix with elements given by

$$c_{ij} = \sum_{k=1}^{n} a_{ik}b_{kj} \quad (i = 1, 2, \ldots, m \text{ and } j = 1, 2, \ldots, p).$$

For example, if $\mathbf{A} = \begin{pmatrix} a_{11} & a_{12} \\ a_{21} & a_{22} \\ a_{31} & a_{32} \end{pmatrix}$ and $\mathbf{B} = \begin{pmatrix} b_{11} & b_{12} & b_{13} \\ b_{21} & b_{22} & b_{23} \end{pmatrix}$, then

$$\mathbf{C} = \mathbf{AB} = \begin{pmatrix} a_{11}b_{11} + a_{12}b_{21} & a_{11}b_{12} + a_{12}b_{22} & a_{11}b_{13} + a_{12}b_{23} \\ a_{21}b_{11} + a_{22}b_{21} & a_{21}b_{12} + a_{22}b_{22} & a_{21}b_{13} + a_{22}b_{23} \\ a_{31}b_{11} + a_{32}b_{21} & a_{31}b_{12} + a_{32}b_{22} & a_{31}b_{13} + a_{32}b_{23} \end{pmatrix}.$$

In most cases, $\mathbf{AB} \neq \mathbf{BA}$. The **power** $\mathbf{A}^n$ of a square matrix $\mathbf{A}$ is formed by multiplying together n matrices $\mathbf{A}$; for example, $\mathbf{A}^3 = \mathbf{AAA}$.

Matrix addition

Two matrices $\mathbf{A}$ and $\mathbf{B}$ can be added only if they have the same size. If $\mathbf{A}$ and $\mathbf{B}$ are $m \times n$ matrices, then $\mathbf{C} = \mathbf{A} + \mathbf{B}$ is also an $m \times n$ matrix with elements given by

$$c_{ij} = a_{ij} + b_{ij} \quad (i = 1, 2, \ldots, m \text{ and } j = 1, 2, \ldots, n).$$

For example, if $\mathbf{A} = \begin{pmatrix} a_{11} & a_{12} & a_{13} \\ a_{21} & a_{22} & a_{23} \end{pmatrix}$ and $\mathbf{B} = \begin{pmatrix} b_{11} & b_{12} & b_{13} \\ b_{21} & b_{22} & b_{23} \end{pmatrix}$, then

$$\mathbf{C} = \mathbf{A} + \mathbf{B} = \begin{pmatrix} a_{11} + b_{11} & a_{12} + b_{12} & a_{13} + b_{13} \\ a_{21} + b_{21} & a_{22} + b_{22} & a_{23} + b_{23} \end{pmatrix}.$$

Scalar multiplication

When a matrix is scalar multiplied by a real number k, each element of the matrix is multiplied by k. For example, if

$$\mathbf{A} = \begin{pmatrix} a_{11} & a_{12} & a_{13} \\ a_{21} & a_{22} & a_{23} \end{pmatrix}, \text{ then } k\mathbf{A} = \begin{pmatrix} ka_{11} & ka_{12} & ka_{13} \\ ka_{21} & ka_{22} & ka_{23} \end{pmatrix}.$$

The matrix $k\mathbf{A}$ is a **scalar multiple** of the matrix $\mathbf{A}$.

General properties of matrices

For any matrices $\mathbf{A}$, $\mathbf{B}$ and $\mathbf{C}$ of appropriate size, and any real number k:

$$\mathbf{A} + \mathbf{B} = \mathbf{B} + \mathbf{A} \qquad (\mathbf{A} + \mathbf{B}) + \mathbf{C} = \mathbf{A} + (\mathbf{B} + \mathbf{C})$$
$$(\mathbf{AB})\mathbf{C} = \mathbf{A}(\mathbf{BC}) \qquad \mathbf{A}(k\mathbf{B}) = (k\mathbf{A})\mathbf{B} = k(\mathbf{AB})$$
$$\mathbf{AB} + \mathbf{AC} = \mathbf{A}(\mathbf{B} + \mathbf{C})$$

Vectors

A **vector** is a matrix with only one column. Elements of a vector $\mathbf{v}$ are often called **components** and are specified as v_i. The size of a vector is the number of components it has.

For vectors $\mathbf{u}$ and $\mathbf{v}$, the vectors $\mathbf{u} + \mathbf{v}$ and $k\mathbf{u}$ are formed according to the definitions for general matrices.

Population modelling

A matrix model for the structure of a population in terms of two interdependent subpopulations J_n and A_n is given by

$$\mathbf{p}_{n+1} = \mathbf{M}\mathbf{p}_n \quad (n = 0, 1, 2, \ldots),$$

where $\mathbf{M}$ is a 2×2 matrix and $\mathbf{p}_n$ is the vector $\begin{pmatrix} J_n \\ A_n \end{pmatrix}$ which gives the subpopulation sizes at n years after a chosen starting time.

The closed-form solution for this model is

$$\mathbf{p}_n = \mathbf{M}^n\mathbf{p}_0 \quad (n = 1, 2, 3, \ldots).$$

Inverting 2 × 2 matrices

The matrix $\mathbf{I} = \begin{pmatrix} 1 & 0 \\ 0 & 1 \end{pmatrix}$ is the 2×2 **identity matrix**. For any 2×2 matrix $\mathbf{A}$,

$$\mathbf{AI} = \mathbf{IA} = \mathbf{A}.$$

If two 2×2 matrices $\mathbf{A}$ and $\mathbf{B}$ have the property that $\mathbf{AB} = \mathbf{I} = \mathbf{BA}$, then $\mathbf{B}$ is the **inverse** of $\mathbf{A}$. The inverse of a matrix $\mathbf{A}$ is usually denoted $\mathbf{A}^{-1}$. The inverse of the general 2×2 matrix $\begin{pmatrix} a & b \\ c & d \end{pmatrix}$ is given by

$$\frac{1}{ad - bc}\begin{pmatrix} d & -b \\ -c & a \end{pmatrix}, \quad \text{provided } ad - bc \neq 0.$$

The **determinant** of a square matrix is a number calculated from its elements. For a 2×2 matrix $\mathbf{A} = \begin{pmatrix} a & b \\ c & d \end{pmatrix}$, the determinant is given by $\det \mathbf{A} = ad - bc$.

Determinant test for invertibility

If the determinant of a matrix $\mathbf{A}$ is not zero, then $\mathbf{A}$ has an inverse and $\mathbf{A}$ is **invertible**.

If the determinant of a matrix $\mathbf{A}$ is zero, then $\mathbf{A}$ does not have an inverse and $\mathbf{A}$ is **non-invertible**.

Solving a pair of simultaneous linear equations using matrices

Write the simultaneous linear equations in matrix form $\mathbf{Ax} = \mathbf{b}$, where $\mathbf{A}$ is the coefficient matrix, $\mathbf{x}$ is the vector of variables and $\mathbf{b}$ is the vector with components equal to the right-hand sides of the equations.

If the matrix $\mathbf{A}$ is invertible, then the solution is given by $\mathbf{x} = \mathbf{A}^{-1}\mathbf{b}$.

MST121 Chapter B3 Modelling with vectors

Vectors can be represented: by 2×1 matrices (column form), by arrows in the (x, y)-plane (geometric form), or by using the Cartesian unit vectors $\mathbf{i}$ and $\mathbf{j}$ (component form).

Arithmetic of vectors in column form

The **sum** of two vectors with the same number of components is formed by adding the corresponding components.
The **scalar multiple** of a vector $\mathbf{a}$ by a real number (scalar) k, denoted by $k\mathbf{a}$, is formed by multiplying each component of $\mathbf{a}$ by k.

Arithmetic of vectors in geometric form

Triangle Rule

To find the sum $\mathbf{a} + \mathbf{b}$ of two vectors $\mathbf{a}$ and $\mathbf{b}$ in geometric form.

1. Choose any point P in the plane.
2. Draw an arrow to represent $\mathbf{a}$, with tail at P and tip at Q, say.
3. Draw an arrow to represent $\mathbf{b}$, with tail at Q and tip at R, say.
4. Draw the arrow with tail at P and tip at R, to complete the triangle PQR. This last arrow represents the vector $\mathbf{a} + \mathbf{b}$.

Parallelogram Rule

To find the sum $\mathbf{a} + \mathbf{b}$ of two vectors $\mathbf{a}$ and $\mathbf{b}$ in geometric form.

1. Choose any point P in the plane.
2. Draw an arrow to represent $\mathbf{a}$, with tail at P and tip at Q, say.
3. Draw an arrow to represent $\mathbf{b}$, with tail at P and tip at S, say.
4. Complete the parallelogram $PQRS$, and draw the arrow with tail at P and tip at R. This last arrow represents the vector $\mathbf{a} + \mathbf{b}$.

Scalar multiplication

If $\mathbf{a}$ is a vector in geometric form and k is a real number, then the scalar multiple $k\mathbf{a}$ has magnitude $|k\mathbf{a}| = |k||\mathbf{a}|$. If k is non-zero, then the direction of $k\mathbf{a}$ is the same as that of $\mathbf{a}$ if $k > 0$, or opposite to that of $\mathbf{a}$ if $k < 0$.

Arithmetic of vectors in component form

The **sum** of two vectors in component form, $\mathbf{a} = a_1\mathbf{i} + a_2\mathbf{j}$ and $\mathbf{b} = b_1\mathbf{i} + b_2\mathbf{j}$, is given by $\mathbf{a} + \mathbf{b} = (a_1 + b_1)\mathbf{i} + (a_2 + b_2)\mathbf{j}$.

The **scalar multiple** of a vector in component form, $\mathbf{a} = a_1\mathbf{i} + a_2\mathbf{j}$, by a real number k, is given by $k\mathbf{a} = ka_1\mathbf{i} + ka_2\mathbf{j}$.

Converting vectors from geometric form to component form

A vector $\mathbf{a}$ in geometric form, with direction θ, has component form

$$\mathbf{a} = |\mathbf{a}|\cos\theta\,\mathbf{i} + |\mathbf{a}|\sin\theta\,\mathbf{j};$$

that is, the $\mathbf{i}$-component of $\mathbf{a}$ is $a_1 = |\mathbf{a}|\cos\theta$ and the $\mathbf{j}$-component of $\mathbf{a}$ is $a_2 = |\mathbf{a}|\sin\theta$.

Converting vectors from component form to geometric form

A vector in component form, $\mathbf{a} = a_1\mathbf{i} + a_2\mathbf{j}$, has magnitude $|\mathbf{a}| = \sqrt{a_1^2 + a_2^2}$. If the vector is non-zero, then its direction, in terms of the angle θ measured anticlockwise from the positive x-axis, is obtained from the figures below.

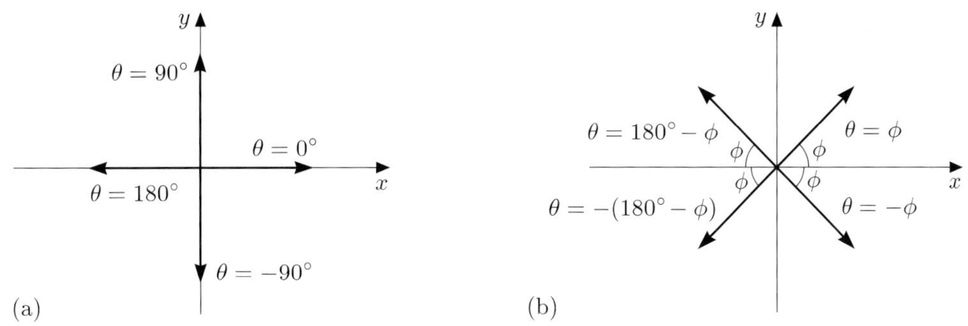

(a) $\mathbf{a}$ is parallel to a coordinate axis (b) $\phi = \arctan(|a_2/a_1|)$

Sine and Cosine Rules

By convention, in a triangle, the vertex labels A, B and C are also used to denote the corresponding angle sizes, while the side lengths opposite the angles are denoted by a, b and c, respectively.

In a triangle ABC, if $a < b$ then $A < B$, and vice versa.

Sine Rule

For any triangle, the side lengths a, b, c and corresponding opposite angles A, B, C are related by the formulas

$$\frac{\sin A}{a} = \frac{\sin B}{b} = \frac{\sin C}{c} \quad \text{or, equivalently,} \quad \frac{a}{\sin A} = \frac{b}{\sin B} = \frac{c}{\sin C}.$$

Cosine Rule

For any triangle, the side lengths a, b, c and corresponding opposite angles A, B, C are related by the formulas

$$a^2 = b^2 + c^2 - 2bc\cos A, \qquad \cos A = \frac{b^2 + c^2 - a^2}{2bc},$$

$$b^2 = c^2 + a^2 - 2ca\cos B, \qquad \cos B = \frac{c^2 + a^2 - b^2}{2ca},$$

$$c^2 = a^2 + b^2 - 2ab\cos C, \qquad \cos C = \frac{a^2 + b^2 - c^2}{2ab}.$$

Equilibrium Condition for forces

If an object is acted upon by n forces, $\mathbf{F}_1, \mathbf{F}_2, \ldots, \mathbf{F}_n$, and remains at rest in the absence of other forces, then the force vectors satisfy the equation

$$\sum_{i=1}^{n} \mathbf{F}_i = \mathbf{F}_1 + \mathbf{F}_2 + \cdots + \mathbf{F}_n = \mathbf{0}.$$

MST121 Chapter C1 Differentiation and modelling

Differentiation

Differentiation is a process which enables you to find: the gradient of a graph, and the rate at which one variable changes with respect to another.

Let f be a function.

◇ The **derivative** $f'(x)$ at a point x in the domain of f is the gradient of the graph of f at $(x, f(x))$, given by

$$f'(x) = \lim_{h \to 0} \left(\frac{f(x+h) - f(x)}{h} \right),$$

provided that this limit exists.

◇ If $y = f(x)$, then $f'(x)$ is the **rate of change** of y with respect to x.

A function is **smooth** if its derivative exists at each point of its domain.

In Leibniz notation, $f'(x)$ is $\dfrac{d}{dx}(f(x))$, or $\dfrac{dy}{dx}$ where $y = f(x)$.

In Newton's notation, $\dfrac{ds}{dt} = \dot{s}$ (used only when differentiating with respect to time).

Table of standard derivatives

Function $f(x)$	Derivative $f'(x)$
c	0
x^n	nx^{n-1}
$\sin(ax)$	$a\cos(ax)$
$\cos(ax)$	$-a\sin(ax)$
e^{ax}	ae^{ax}
$\ln(ax)$ $(ax > 0)$	$1/x$ $(ax > 0)$

Sum and Constant Multiple Rules

If k is a function with rule of the form $k(x) = f(x) + g(x)$, where f and g are smooth functions, then k is smooth and

$$k'(x) = f'(x) + g'(x).$$

If k is a function with rule of the form $k(x) = cf(x)$, where f is a smooth function and c is a constant, then k is smooth and

$$k'(x) = cf'(x).$$

Product Rule

If k is a function with rule of the form $k(x) = f(x)g(x)$, where f and g are smooth functions, then k is smooth and

$$k'(x) = f'(x)g(x) + f(x)g'(x).$$

In Leibniz notation, if $y = uv$, where $u = f(x)$ and $v = g(x)$, then

$$\frac{dy}{dx} = \frac{du}{dx}v + u\frac{dv}{dx}.$$

Quotient Rule

If k is a function with rule of the form $k(x) = f(x)/g(x)$, where f and g are smooth functions, then k is smooth and

$$k'(x) = \frac{g(x)f'(x) - f(x)g'(x)}{(g(x))^2}.$$

In Leibniz notation, if $y = u/v$, where $u = f(x)$ and $v = g(x) \neq 0$, then

$$\frac{dy}{dx} = \frac{1}{v^2}\left(v\frac{du}{dx} - u\frac{dv}{dx}\right).$$

Composite Rule

If k is a function with rule of the form $k(x) = g(f(x))$, where f and g are smooth functions, then k is smooth and

$$k'(x) = g'(f(x))f'(x).$$

In Leibniz notation (Chain Rule), if $y = g(u)$, where $u = f(x)$, then

$$\frac{dy}{dx} = \frac{dy}{du}\frac{du}{dx}.$$

Increasing/Decreasing Criterion

Let I be an open interval in the domain of a smooth function f.

- ◇ If $f'(x) > 0$ for all x in I, then f is increasing on I.
- ◇ If $f'(x) < 0$ for all x in I, then f is decreasing on I.

Stationary points

Let f be a smooth function. The function f has a **stationary point** at $x = x_0$ if $f'(x_0) = 0$. The corresponding point $(x_0, f(x_0))$ on the graph of f is also called a stationary point.

First Derivative Test

To identify the local maxima and local minima of a smooth function f using the First Derivative Test proceed as follows.

1. Find the stationary points of f.
2. For each stationary point x_0,
   (a) choose points x_L to the left of x_0 and x_R to the right of x_0, such that the interval $[x_L, x_R]$ lies in the domain of f and there are no stationary points between x_L and x_0, nor between x_0 and x_R, and then calculate $f'(x_L)$ and $f'(x_R)$;
   (b) classify x_0 as follows:
   - ◇ if $f'(x_L) > 0$ and $f'(x_R) < 0$, then f has a local maximum at x_0;
   - ◇ if $f'(x_L) < 0$ and $f'(x_R) > 0$, then f has a local minimum at x_0;
   - ◇ if $f'(x_L)$ and $f'(x_R)$ have the same sign, then f has neither a local maximum nor a local minimum at x_0.

Second Derivative Test

Suppose that x_0 is a stationary point of a smooth function f; that is, $f'(x_0) = 0$.

- ◇ If $f''(x_0) < 0$, then f has a local maximum at x_0.
- ◇ If $f''(x_0) > 0$, then f has a local minimum at x_0.

Optimisation Procedure

To find the greatest (or least) value of a smooth function f on a closed interval I within the domain of f, proceed as follows.

1. Find the stationary points of f.
2. Evaluate f at each of the endpoints of I and at each of the stationary points inside I.
3. Choose the greatest (or least) of the function values found in Step 2.

MST121 Chapter C2 Integration and modelling

Integration

The function F is an **integral** of the function f if $F' = f$. The **indefinite integral** of $f(x)$ is

$$\int f(x)\,dx = F(x) + c,$$

where F is an integral of f and c is an arbitrary constant, also called the **constant of integration**.

The **definite integral** of a continuous function f from a to b, denoted by

$$\int_a^b f(x)\,dx,$$

is defined to be

$$[F(x)]_a^b = F(b) - F(a),$$

where F is any integral of f.

Table of indefinite integrals

Function $f(x)$		Integral $\int f(x)\,dx$
a	(constant)	$ax + c$
x^n	$(n \neq -1)$	$\dfrac{1}{n+1}x^{n+1} + c$
$\dfrac{1}{x}$	$(x > 0)$	$\ln x + c$
e^{ax}		$\dfrac{1}{a}e^{ax} + c$
$\cos(ax)$		$\dfrac{1}{a}\sin(ax) + c$
$\sin(ax)$		$-\dfrac{1}{a}\cos(ax) + c$

Rules for integration

The **Sum Rule** for integrals is

$$\int (f(x) + g(x))\,dx = \int f(x)\,dx + \int g(x)\,dx.$$

The **Constant Multiple Rule** for integrals is

$$\int bf(x)\,dx = b\int f(x)\,dx.$$

The combined Sum and Constant Multiple Rule is

$$\int (af(x) + bg(x))\,dx = a\int f(x)\,dx + b\int g(x)\,dx.$$

Double-angle formulas

$\sin(2\theta) = 2\sin\theta\cos\theta$

$\cos(2\theta) = \cos^2\theta - \sin^2\theta = 2\cos^2\theta - 1 = 1 - 2\sin^2\theta$

Two integration formulas

$$\int (f(x))^n\, f'(x)\,dx = \frac{1}{n+1}(f(x))^{n+1} + c \quad (n \neq -1)$$

$$\int \frac{f'(x)}{f(x)}\,dx = \ln(f(x)) + c \quad (f(x) > 0)$$

Modelling motion

The SI units for kinematic quantities are as follows.

- ◇ Time is measured in seconds (s).
- ◇ Position is measured in metres (m).
- ◇ Velocity is measured in metres per second (m s^{-1}).
- ◇ Acceleration is measured in metres per second per second (m s^{-2}).

Time t, position s, velocity v and acceleration a are related by the equations

$$v = \frac{ds}{dt} \quad \text{and} \quad a = \frac{dv}{dt}.$$

The following formulas apply for the motion of a particle along a straight line with constant acceleration a, if at time $t = 0$ the particle has velocity v_0 and position s_0.

- ◇ The velocity v of the particle is given by

  $$v = at + v_0.$$

- ◇ The position s of the particle is given by

  $$s = \tfrac{1}{2}at^2 + v_0 t + s_0.$$

- ◇ The velocity and position of the particle are related by the equation

  $$v^2 - 2as = v_0^2 - 2as_0.$$

Finding the area under a graph

If $f(x)$ is a continuous function that takes no negative values for $a \leq x \leq b$, then the area of the region bounded by the graph of $y = f(x)$, the x-axis, and the lines $x = a$ and $x = b$, is equal to the definite integral

$$\int_a^b f(x)\, dx.$$

Fundamental Theorem of Calculus

If f is a function which is continuous on the interval $[a, b]$, then

$$\int_a^b f(x)\, dx = \lim_{N \to \infty} \left[\sum_{i=0}^{N-1} h f(a + ih) \right], \quad \text{where } h = \frac{b-a}{N}.$$

MST121 Chapter C3 Differential equations and modelling

Differential equations

A **differential equation** is an equation that relates an independent variable, x say, a dependent variable, y say, and one or more derivatives of y with respect to x. The **order** of a differential equation is the order of the highest derivative that appears in the equation. A **first-order** differential equation involves the first derivative, dy/dx, and no higher derivatives.

A **solution** of a differential equation is a function $y = F(x)$ (or a more general equation relating x and y) for which the differential equation is satisfied. The **general solution** of a differential equation is the set of all possible solutions of the equation. It usually involves one or more arbitrary constants. A **particular solution** of a differential equation is a single solution of the equation, which consists of a relationship between the dependent and independent variables that contains no arbitrary constant.

An **initial condition** associated with a first-order differential equation requires that the dependent variable y takes a specified value, b say, when the independent variable x has a given value, a say. This is often written as

$$y = b \text{ when } x = a, \quad \text{or as} \quad y(a) = b.$$

The numbers a and b are called **initial values** for x and y, respectively. The combination of a first-order differential equation and an initial condition is called an **initial-value problem**. The solution of an initial-value problem is a particular solution of the differential equation which also satisfies the initial condition.

Direct integration

The general solution of the differential equation $dy/dx = f(x)$ is the indefinite integral

$$y = \int f(x)\, dx = F(x) + c,$$

where $F(x)$ is any integral of $f(x)$ and c is an arbitrary constant. Any initial condition

$$y = b \text{ when } x = a, \quad \text{that is,} \quad y(a) = b,$$

enables a value for the arbitrary constant c to be found. The corresponding particular solution satisfies both the differential equation and the initial condition.

Implicit differentiation

If y is a function of x and $H(y) = F(x)$, then $H'(y)\dfrac{dy}{dx} = F'(x)$.

Separation of variables

The method applies to differential equations of the form $dy/dx = f(x)g(y)$.

1. Divide both sides by $g(y)$, for $g(y) \neq 0$, to obtain
$$\frac{1}{g(y)}\frac{dy}{dx} = f(x).$$
2. Integrate both sides with respect to x. The outcome is
$$\int \frac{1}{g(y)}\,dy = \int f(x)\,dx.$$
3. Carry out the two integrations, introducing *one* arbitrary constant, to obtain the general solution in implicit form. If possible, manipulate the resulting equation to make y the subject, thus expressing the general solution in explicit form.

Modelling growth and decay

The differential equation $dy/dx = Ky$, where K is a constant, has the general solution $y = Ae^{Kx}$, where A is an arbitrary constant.

The process of radioactive decay, that is, the change in mass m of a radioactive substance that is present at time t, can be modelled by the initial-value problem

$$\frac{dm}{dt} = -km \quad (m > 0), \qquad m = m_0 \text{ when } t = 0.$$

Here k is a positive constant, called the **decay constant**, and m_0 is the initial mass of the substance. This initial-value problem has the solution

$$m = m_0e^{-kt}.$$

The **half-life** T of a radioactive substance is the time it takes for the mass of radioactive substance to diminish to half its original amount. In the model, we have $T = (\ln 2)/k$. The value of the decay constant k can be estimated from data by plotting $\ln(m/m_0)$ against t. This should approximate a line through the origin with gradient $-k$.

The process of population change, that is, the change in the population size P over time t, can be modelled by the initial-value problem

$$\frac{dP}{dt} = KP \quad (P > 0), \qquad P = P_0 \text{ when } t = 0.$$

Here K is a constant, called the **proportionate growth rate**, and P_0 is the initial population size. This initial-value problem has the solution

$$P = P_0e^{Kt}.$$

If $K < 0$, then the population is decreasing and the half-life of the population can be defined as for radioactive decay. If $K > 0$, then the population is increasing and the **doubling time** T of the population is the time it takes for the population to double in size. In the model, we have $T = (\ln 2)/K$. The value of the proportionate growth rate K can be estimated from data using a log-linear plot of $\ln P$ against t. This should approximate a line which crosses the $(\ln P)$-axis at $\ln P_0$ and has gradient K.

Euler's method

Euler's method for solving the initial-value problem

$$\frac{dy}{dx} = f(x, y), \quad y(x_0) = y_0$$

is described by the pair of recurrence relations

$$x_{n+1} = x_n + h, \quad y_{n+1} = y_n + hf(x_n, y_n) \quad (n = 0, 1, 2, \ldots),$$

where h is the step size between the successive values of x at which solution estimates are calculated. Each calculated value y_n is an estimate of the corresponding 'true solution' y at $x = x_n$; that is, y_n is an estimate of $y(x_n)$. The sequence of estimates depends on the choice of both the step size h and the overall number of steps N. Decreasing h, while increasing N to cover the same range of x-values, leads to progressively improved estimates for the solution values, and with a small enough step size, any desired level of accuracy can be achieved.

MST121 Chapter D1 Chance

Probability

For any event E, $0 \leq P(E) \leq 1$.

If an event E never happens, then $P(E) = 0$.

If an event E is certain to happen, then $P(E) = 1$.

If an experiment has N equally-likely possible outcomes, and $n(E)$ is the number of these outcomes that give rise to an event E, then

$$P(E) = \frac{n(E)}{N};$$

that is, $P(E)$ is equal to the number of outcomes for which the event E occurs divided by the total number of possible outcomes.

If E is an event and not-E is the opposite event (that E does not occur), then

$$P(E) + P(\text{not-}E) = 1,$$

or, equivalently,

$$P(E) = 1 - P(\text{not-}E).$$

Two events are **independent** of each other if the occurrence (or not) of one is not influenced by whether or not the other occurs.

The **multiplication rule for independent events** states that if E and F are independent events, then

$$P(E \text{ and } F) = P(E) \times P(F).$$

Geometric distributions

If a sequence of trials of an experiment is carried out and the probability of success in each trial is p $(0 < p < 1)$ independently of the results of earlier trials, then X, the number of trials required to obtain a success, has a **geometric distribution**. The probability function of X is given by

$$P(X = j) = (1 - p)^{j-1}p, \quad j = 1, 2, 3, \ldots.$$

The mean number of trials required to obtain a success is $1/p$.

Probability distributions

The **mean** of the probability distribution of a discrete random variable X is denoted by μ and is defined to be

$$\mu = \sum_j j \times P(X = j),$$

where the summation is over all values j which X can take, that is, for which $P(X = j) > 0$.

The corresponding formula for the mean of a continuous random variable X with probability density function f is

$$\mu = \int_{-\infty}^{\infty} x\, f(x)\, dx.$$

MST121 Chapter D2 Modelling variation

The **variance** of a random variable X or of a probability distribution is the mean of the values $(x-\mu)^2$, where the mean is taken over all values x that X can take. The **standard deviation** of a random variable or of a probability distribution is the square root of the variance.

When a probability distribution is used to model the variation in a population, the mean of the distribution is called the **population mean**, and the standard deviation is called the **population standard deviation**. The population mean and the population standard deviation are examples of **population parameters**.

Sample statistics and population parameters

For a sample of n observations $x_1, x_2, \dots, x_n$, the **sample mean** $\overline{x}$ is given by

$$\overline{x} = \frac{1}{n}(x_1 + x_2 + \cdots + x_n) = \frac{1}{n}\sum_{i=1}^{n} x_i,$$

and the **sample standard deviation** s is given by

$$s = \sqrt{\frac{1}{n-1}\sum_{i=1}^{n}(x_i - \overline{x})^2}.$$

The sample mean and sample standard deviation are examples of **sample statistics**. In general, given a sample of data from a population, the sample mean $\overline{x}$ is used to estimate the population mean μ, and the sample standard deviation s is used to estimate the population standard deviation σ.

Normal distributions

A **normal distribution** is a continuous probability distribution. Probabilities are calculated by finding areas under a normal curve, which has the following typical shape.

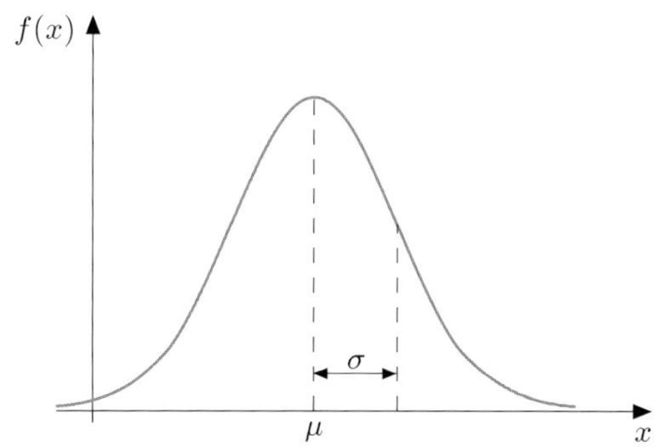

The probability density function of a normal distribution is the function f, where $y = f(x)$ is the equation of the normal curve. It is defined for all real values of x. The equation of a normal curve contains two parameters, μ and σ: μ is the mean of the distribution, and σ is its standard deviation. The curve is symmetric about its peak, which occurs at $x = \mu$. The normal distribution with mean 0 and standard deviation 1 is called the **standard normal distribution**.

If a normal distribution is used to model the variation in a population, then, according to the model, the proportion of the population within k standard deviations of the mean is the same whatever the values of the mean μ and the standard deviation σ. In particular, approximately 95% of the population are within 1.96 standard deviations of the mean (that is, between $\mu - 1.96\sigma$ and $\mu + 1.96\sigma$).

MST121 Chapter D3 Estimating

Sampling distributions, the Central Limit Theorem and confidence intervals

The sampling distribution of the mean for samples of size n from a population with mean μ and standard deviation σ has mean μ and standard deviation $\sigma/\sqrt{n}$. These results hold for any sample size.

The standard deviation of the sampling distribution of the mean is called the **standard error of the mean** and is denoted by SE.

The **Central Limit Theorem** states that, for large sample sizes (at least 25), the sampling distribution of the mean for samples of size n from a population with mean μ and standard deviation σ may be approximated by a normal distribution with mean μ and standard deviation

$$SE = \frac{\sigma}{\sqrt{n}}.$$

Given a sample of size n from a population, a **95% confidence interval** for the population mean μ is given by

$$\left(\overline{x} - 1.96\frac{s}{\sqrt{n}}, \overline{x} + 1.96\frac{s}{\sqrt{n}}\right),$$

where $\overline{x}$ is the sample mean and s is the sample standard deviation. The sample size n must be at least 25.

MST121 Chapter D4 Further investigations

Summary statistics and boxplots

The **median** is essentially the middle value of a batch of data when the values are placed in order of increasing size. If the batch size is odd, then the median is the middle value. If the batch size is even, then the median is the mean of the middle two values.

The **lower quartile**, which is denoted by $Q1$, is the median of the values to the left of the median.

The **upper quartile**, which is denoted by $Q3$, is the median of the values to the right of the median.

The **interquartile range** is the difference between the upper quartile and the lower quartile.

The **range** is the difference between the maximum value and the minimum value.

A **boxplot** is a diagram for representing a batch of data. A typical boxplot is shown below.

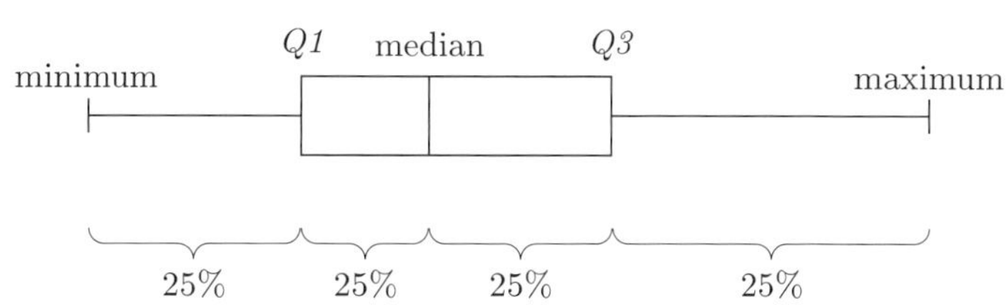

The box extends from the lower quartile to the upper quartile, and a vertical line is drawn through the box at the median. The whiskers extend from the ends of the box to the minimum and maximum values in the batch of data.

Hypothesis testing

There are three stages involved in a hypothesis test:

1. Set up the null and alternative hypotheses.
2. Calculate the test statistic.
3. Report conclusions.

The **two-sample z-test** is a hypothesis test which may be used when a sample of at least 25 observations is available from each of two populations. It may be used to investigate whether there is a difference between the means of the populations. The three stages involved in carrying out the two-sample z-test are outlined below.

Stage 1: Hypotheses

Set up the null and alternative hypotheses:

$$H_0 : \mu_A = \mu_B,$$
$$H_1 : \mu_A \neq \mu_B,$$

where μ_A and μ_B are the means of populations A and B, respectively.

Stage 2: The test statistic

Calculate the test statistic

$$z = \frac{\overline{x}_A - \overline{x}_B}{ESE},$$

where

$$ESE = \sqrt{\frac{s_A^2}{n_A} + \frac{s_B^2}{n_B}},$$

$\overline{x}_A$ and $\overline{x}_B$ are the sample means, s_A and s_B are the sample standard deviations, and n_A and n_B are the sizes of the samples from A and B, respectively.

Stage 3: Conclusions

- ◇ If $z \leq -1.96$ or $z \geq 1.96$, then H_0 is rejected at the 5% significance level in favour of the alternative hypothesis.
- ◇ If $-1.96 < z < 1.96$, then H_0 is not rejected at the 5% significance level.

The conclusion should be expressed in terms of the hypothesis being tested.

The quantity ESE in the test statistic for the two-sample z-test is the estimated standard error of the difference between two sample means; that is, it is the estimated value of the standard deviation of the sampling distribution of the difference between two sample means.

Fitting lines to data

The **least squares fit line** for a set of data points is the line that minimises the sum of the squared residuals for the data set. It is also known as the **regression line** of y on x. It may be used to predict values of y, the **dependent variable**, for values of x, the **explanatory variable**, but not vice versa. It should be used only to predict y-values for x-values that are within, or just outside, the range of values of x represented in the data.